Test Your Bible IQ

Test Your Bible IQ

Christopher O. Edwards

Produced by
The Philip Lief Group, Inc.

BARNES
&NOBLE
BOOKS
NEW YORK

1999 Barnes & Noble Books

ISBN 0-7607-1062-7

Book design by Margaret Trejo

Printed and bound in the United States of America

02 03 M 9 8 7 6 5 4

FG

For Becky

Acknowledgments

I want to acknowledge and thank several people for making this project possible. Thanks go to The Philip Lief Group for conceiving the idea and inviting me to be part of it. Jim Pomager deserves special notice. Thanks, Jim, for your editorial guidance, wisdom, and availability. I needed your help and have enjoyed our friendship.

I want to thank my children. Tim, Andrew, and Katie made good guinea pigs around the dinner table as I tried to see if questions were too hard or too easy. They did not complain (much) as it became clear that Dad's summer project this year would keep him from finishing his summer project from last year—the tree house. Maybe next year, kids—if you pay me!

I also want to thank my wife, Becky. She often did double parental duty as I disappeared at every opportunity to a desk in the basement to write a few more questions. On more than one occasion, she came down to discuss an important family matter only to have her Bible IQ tested with the latest set of questions. I am thankful for her patience and graceful companionship.

Contents

CONTENTS

Introduction

I will be honest with you. When I first signed on to this project, I was in it for the money. Specifically, I was looking for a way to pay for my children's orthodontia. Like most church pastors, I am not exactly hauling in the big bucks. So when this opportunity came up, with the chance of paying for a set of braces and maybe getting a start on set number two, I signed on the dotted line.

As the project progressed, I found my motives changing. My son's silver smile certainly reminded me of my original intent, but I also had a growing desire to see this book become a useful—and, of course, entertaining—tool for people. I wanted it to be more than just another trivia book.

This desire guided the selection of questions. As you can imagine, a big book like the Bible contains enough information for an infinite number. I had to be selective, and so most of the questions involve events and people central to the Bible's story. The questions that are not central are at least interesting. I even incorporated questions from a "Bible Content" exam I had to pass in order to be ordained. Just think, if you answer lots of questions correctly, you know as much as many ministers!

I also selected questions with varying levels of difficulty. Some are impossible for all but the experts. On the other hand, some of the questions were easy for my nine-year-old daughter.

I chose to use the New International Version of the Bible as the basis for the questions and answers because it is the most widely used translation in America today. There are two exceptions to this rule. In Chapter 15, the answers in "Straight to the Source: Old Testament" and "Straight to the Source: New Testament" are words and phrases that have made their way into our everyday language via the King James version of the Bible. If you want to look up the references to these answers, check a King James version of the Bible, not a New International Version.

If you work through the book, and perhaps use the references to read more about the answers, your Bible literacy will improve dramatically. Bible literacy is quite a useful thing, for your faith, your cultural understanding, and, well, for just impressing your friends. One of my ancestors said, "Every man of common understanding who can read, may, if he please, become well acquainted with the Scriptures. And what an excellent attainment would this be!" (Jonathan Edwards, 1703–1758).

Besides being useful, I hope this book will be fun. As I wrote questions, I tried to imagine people using the book around the dinner table, or during a long drive in the car, or as an introduction to a Sunday school class, or as a party game. I held back very little of the playfulness that came to mind as I wrote the questions. Some came from me, some from one of my kids looking over my shoulder. I hope it brings a smile here or a chuckle there, but not offense. The Bible is a serious book, but seriousness and fun need not be mutually exclusive.

The Bible is the most important book ever written. If you read it and take it to heart, you will find yourself a changed person. Dwight D. Eisenhower once said, "To read the Bible is to take a trip to a fair land where the spirit is strengthened and faith renewed." I hope this book proves to be a helpful and enjoyable way for you to get into the Bible, and for the Bible to get into you.

1

FIRST
THINGS
FIRST

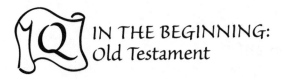

IN THE BEGINNING:
Old Testament

Name the books of the Old Testament that begin with these lines.

1. "The words of the Teacher, son of David, king in Jerusalem: Meaningless! Meaningless!"

2. "Let him kiss me with the kisses of his mouth—for your love is more delightful than wine."

3. "After the death of Moses the servant of the Lord . . ."

4. "In the beginning, God created the heavens and the earth."

5. "After the death of Joshua, the Israelites asked the Lord, 'Who will be the first to go up and fight for us against the Canaanites?'"

6. "In the days when the judges ruled there was a famine in the land."

7. "How deserted lies the city, once so full of people."

8. "When King David was old and well advanced in years, he could not keep warm even when they put covers over him."

9. "In the first year of Cyrus king of Persia, in order to fulfill the word of the Lord spoken by Jeremiah . . ."

10. "The Lord called to Moses and spoke to him from the Tent of Meeting."

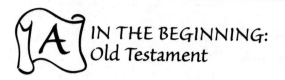

IN THE BEGINNING:
Old Testament

1. Ecclesiastes

2. Song of Songs

3. Joshua

4. Genesis

5. Judges

6. Ruth

7. Lamentations

8. 1 Kings

9. Ezra

10. Leviticus

IN THE BEGINNING:
New Testament

Name the books of the New Testament that begin with these lines.

1. "The beginning of the gospel about Jesus Christ, the Son of God."

2. "A record of the genealogy of Jesus Christ the son of David, the son of Abraham."

3. "In the past God spoke to our forefathers through the prophets at many times and in various ways."

4. "The revelation of Jesus Christ, which God gave him to show his servants what must soon take place."

5. "Many have undertaken to draw up an account of the things that have been fulfilled among us."

6. "In the beginning was the Word, and the Word was with God, and the Word was God."

7. "The elder, to my dear friend Gaius, whom I love in the truth."

8. "In my former book, Theophilus, I wrote about all that Jesus began to do and to teach."

9. "Paul, called to be an apostle of Christ Jesus by the will of God, and our brother Sosthenes . . ."

IN THE BEGINNING:
New Testament

1. Mark

2. Matthew

3. Hebrews

4. Revelation

5. Luke

6. John

7. 3 John

8. Acts

9. 1 Corinthians

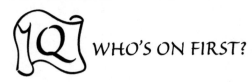 WHO'S ON FIRST?

Test your Bible IQ with these questions about Bible firsts.

1. What feast was celebrated with the firstfruits of the crop?

2. Who was the first Christian convert in the province of Asia?

3. Who is the firstfruits of those who have fallen asleep?

4. What were the Corinthians to lay aside on the first day of the week?

5. What is the first fruit of the Spirit?

6. What shall the first be?

7. What are Jesus' disciples to seek first?

8. Where were Jesus' disciples first called Christians?

9. Who had the first fight?

10. Who made the first clothes?

WHO'S ON FIRST?

1. Feast of Harvest (Exodus 23:16)

2. Epenetus (Romans 16:5)

3. Jesus (1 Corinthians 15:20)

4. money for the collection (1 Corinthians 16:2)

5. love (Galatians 5:22)

6. last (Matthew 19:20)

7. the kingdom of God and his righteousness (Matthew 6:33)

8. Antioch (Acts 11:26)

9. Cain and Abel (Genesis 4:8)

10. God (Genesis 3:21)

LET THERE BE . . .

Test your knowledge of the creation story with these questions.

1. What was hovering over the waters on the first day
   of creation?
   a. the Glory of God
   b. seagulls
   c. the Spirit of God
   d. an Angel of God

2. On what day was the sun created?
   a. Sunday
   b. first day
   c. second day
   d. fourth day

3. On what day did dry ground appear?
   a. first day
   b. second day
   c. third day
   d. fourth day

4. On what day did God make Adam and Eve?
   a. third day
   b. fourth day
   c. fifth day
   d. sixth day

5. What did God give Adam and Eve for food?
   a. manna
   b. only meat
   c. meat and plants
   d. only plants

LET THERE BE . . .

1.   c. the Spirit of God (Genesis 1:2)

2.   d. fourth day (Genesis 1:16)

3.   c. third day (Genesis 1:9)

4.   d. sixth day (Genesis 1:27)

5.   d. only plants (Genesis 1:29)

MORE LET THERE BE . . .

Test your knowledge of the creation story with these questions.

1. From what tree were Adam and Eve not allowed to eat?
   a. tree of life
   b. giving tree
   c. tree of knowledge of good and evil
   d. tree of wisdom and happiness

2. What watered the Garden of Eden?
   a. rain
   b. a river
   c. a pond
   d. an angel

3. Before God made Eve, what did He do to Adam?
   a. He clothed him with fig leaves.
   b. He gave him a credit card.
   c. He woke him up.
   d. He put him to sleep.

4. Who named the animals?
   a. God
   b. Adam
   c. Eve
   d. They came with names.

5. Eve was made from what part of Adam's body?
   a. rib
   b. nose
   c. thigh
   d. heart

MORE LET THERE BE . . .

1. c. tree of knowledge of good and evil (Genesis 2:17)

2. b. a river (Genesis 2:10)

3. d. He put him to sleep. (Genesis 2:21)

4. b. Adam (Genesis 2:20)

5. a. rib (Genesis 2:21)

FIRST IN LINE

On the left is a list of firstborn sons, and on the right, a list of their parents. Can you match the firstborn with his proud parent?

1. ___ Esau   a. Canaan

2. ___ Reuben   b. Joseph

3. ___ Eliphaz   c. Jacob

4. ___ Er   d. Adam

5. ___ Manasseh   e. Aaron

6. ___ Nabab   f. Esau

7. ___ Jesus   g. Isaac

8. ___ Sidon   h. Judah

9. ___ Shem   i. Mary

10. ___ Cain   j. Noah

FIRST IN LINE

1. g. Isaac (Genesis 27:19)

2. c. Jacob (Genesis 35:23)

3. f. Esau (Genesis 36:15)

4. h. Judah (Genesis 38:6)

5. b. Joseph (Genesis 41:51)

6. e. Aaron (Numbers 3:2)

7. i. Mary (Luke 2:2)

8. a. Canaan (Genesis 10:15)

9. j. Noah (Genesis 9:18)

10. d. Adam (Genesis 4:1)

WHO CAME FIRST?

Arrange the following people in the order they appear in the Bible.

1. __		a.	Jacob
2. __		b.	Samson
3. __		c.	Abraham
4. __		d.	Joshua
5. __		e.	Adam
6. __		f.	Joseph
7. __		g.	Noah
8. __		h.	Samuel
9. __		i.	Isaac
10. __		j.	Moses

WHO CAME FIRST?

1. e. Adam (Genesis 2:20)

2. g. Noah (Genesis 5:29)

3. c. Abraham (Genesis 17:5)

4. i. Isaac (Genesis 17:19)

5. a. Jacob (Genesis 25:26)

6. f. Joseph (Genesis 30:24)

7. j. Moses (Exodus 2:10)

8. d. Joshua (Exodus 17:9)

9. b. Samson (Judges 13:28)

10. h. Samuel (Numbers 34:20)

THE RETURN OF WHO CAME FIRST?

Arrange the following people in the order they appear in the Bible.

1. ___		a.	Rehoboam
2. ___		b.	David
3. ___		c.	Nehemiah
4. ___		d.	Elisha
5. ___		e.	Ruth
6. ___		f.	Jehoiachin
7. ___		g.	Solomon
8. ___		h.	Saul
9. ___		i.	Elijah
10. ___		j.	Ezra

THE RETURN OF WHO CAME FIRST?

1. e. Ruth (Ruth 1:4)

2. h. Saul (1 Samuel 9:2)

3. b. David (1 Samuel 16:13)

4. g. Solomon (2 Samuel 5:14)

5. a. Rehoboam (1 Kings 11:43)

6. i. Elijah (1 Kings 17:1)

7. d. Elisha (1 Kings 19:16)

8. f. Jehoiachin (2 Kings 24:6)

9. j. Ezra (Ezra 7:1)

10. c. Nehemiah (Nehemiah 1:1)

11

BIBLE
BASICS

JUST THE FACTS:
Old Testament

Test your knowledge of the Old Testament with these questions.

1. How many books are there in the Old Testament?

2. What is the longest book in the Old Testament?

3. What is the shortest book in the Old Testament?

4. What is the first book in the Old Testament?

5. What is the last book in the Old Testament?

6. Who is the oldest man in the Old Testament?

7. What man is mentioned more often than anyone else in the Old Testament?

8. Which six books of the Old Testament tell the stories of Israel's kings?

9. What book in the Old Testament is composed primarily of hymns, songs, and poetry?

10. What five books are called "The Book of Moses"?

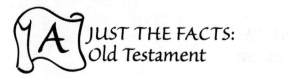

JUST THE FACTS:
Old Testament

1. 39

2. Psalms

3. Obadiah

4. Genesis

5. Malachi

6. Methuselah, who lived to be 969 (Genesis 5:27)

7. David

8. 1 Samuel, 2 Samuel, 1 Kings, 2 Kings, 1 Chronicles, 2 Chronicles

9. Psalms

10. Genesis, Exodus, Leviticus, Numbers, Deuteronomy (Ezra 6:18)

JUST THE FACTS:
New Testament

Test your knowledge of the New Testament with these questions.

1. How many books are there in the New Testament?

2. What are the names of the Gospels—the first four books of the New Testament?

3. What is the last book of the New Testament?

4. What is the longest book in the New Testament?

5. What is the shortest book in the New Testament?

6. What Old Testament book is referred to most frequently in the New Testament?

7. What Old Testament verse is most frequently quoted in the New Testament?

8. What is the shortest verse in the New Testament?

9. Who wrote more New Testament books than anyone else?

10. What person is mentioned more often than anyone else in the New Testament?

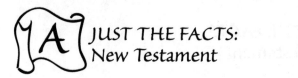

JUST THE FACTS:
New Testament

1. 27

2. Matthew, Mark, Luke, John

3. Revelation

4. Acts

5. 3 John

6. Isaiah (419 times)

7. Psalm 110:1 (18 times)

8. "Jesus wept." (John 11:35)

9. Paul

10. Jesus

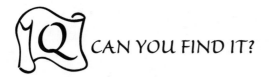 CAN YOU FIND IT?

For each of these important events, identify the book of the Bible in which the event is documented.

1. Peter visits Cornelius, and sees that God accepts both Jews and Gentiles who believe.

2. The people of Israel want a king appointed so that they can be like the surrounding nations.

3. The people of Israel worship a golden calf made by Aaron.

4. Paul visits Jerusalem and is arrested for defiling the temple.

5. Twelve men explore the land of Canaan, but only Caleb and Joshua are confident that God's people can possess the land.

6. Nebuchadnezzar goes temporarily insane, but is later healed when he gives praise to God.

7. Cyrus permits the Jews to return to Jerusalem and gives them silver and gold utensils for the temple.

8. Elijah is taken up to heaven in a whirlwind, and Elisha receives a "double portion of his spirit."

9. God commands circumcision as a sign of his covenant with Abraham.

10. Elihu lectures his friend on the reason for his suffering.

CAN YOU FIND IT?

1. Acts (Acts 10)

2. 1 Samuel (1 Samuel 8)

3. Exodus (Exodus 32)

4. Acts (Acts 21)

5. Numbers (Numbers 13)

6. Daniel (Daniel 4)

7. Ezra (Ezra 1)

8. 2 Kings (2 Kings 2)

9. Genesis (Genesis 17)

10. Job (Job 32)

GET IN LINE:
Old Testament

Arrange the following Old Testament events in their correct historical order.

1. ___

2. ___

3. ___

4. ___

5. ___

6. ___

7. ___

8. ___

9. ___

10. ___

a. The people of Judah are exiled to Babylon.

b. Moses leads God's people out of Egypt.

c. Elijah challenges the prophets of Baal on Mount Carmel.

d. Haggai urges God's people to complete the temple.

e. Saul is killed; David becomes king over Judah.

f. Noah builds the ark.

g. Joseph is reunited with his brothers.

h. Joshua leads in the capture of Jericho.

i. Isaac is born to Sarah.

j. God gives the Ten Commandments.

GET IN LINE: Old Testament

1. f. Noah builds the ark. (Genesis 6)

2. i. Isaac is born to Sarah. (Genesis 21)

3. g. Joseph is reunited with his brothers. (Genesis 42)

4. b. Moses leads God's people out of Egypt. (Exodus 12)

5. j. God gives the Ten Commandments. (Exodus 20)

6. h. Joshua leads in the capture of Jericho. (Joshua 6)

7. e. Saul is killed; David becomes king over Judah. (2 Samuel 1)

8. c. Elijah challenges the prophets of Baal on Mount Carmel. (1 Kings 18)

9. a. The people of Judah are exiled to Babylon. (2 Kings 25)

10. d. Haggai urges God's people to complete the temple. (Ezra 5)

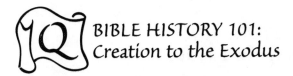

BIBLE HISTORY 101:
Creation to the Exodus

Are the following statements about key events in Bible history true or false? For extra credit, correct the false statements.

1. In the beginning, God created the heavens and the earth.

2. The devil tricked Adam into eating the fruit, and Adam then gave some to Eve.

3. God told Noah to bring only two of each kind of animal aboard the ark.

4. People living on the plain of Shinar tried to build a city with a tower reaching to the heavens. The city was called Babel.

5. The Lord came to Abram and said, "Leave your country, your people and your father's household and go to the land of Egypt."

6. God made a covenant with Abram and warned him that he would be like a wandering Aramean with no place to lay his head.

7. Jacob's brothers sold him into slavery in the land of Egypt.

8. The descendants of Joseph were enslaved in Egypt because the new king did not know about Joseph.

9. While Moses was tending the flock of his father-in-law, Jethro, God spoke to him from a burning bush.

10. God tried to convince Pharaoh to free the people of Israel by inflicting twelve plagues on Egypt.

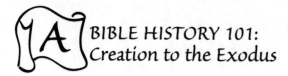

BIBLE HISTORY 101:
Creation to the Exodus

1. True (Genesis 1:1)

2. False—The devil tricked Eve, and she gave the fruit to Adam. (Genesis 3)

3. False—God told Noah to bring seven of every kind of clean animal and seven of every kind of bird. (Genesis 7:2, 3)

4. True (Genesis 11)

5. False—God told Abram to go to the land He would show him. (Genesis 12:1)

6. False—God made a covenant with Abram and promised him the land of Canaan. (Genesis 13:11–16)

7. False—Joseph was sold into slavery. (Genesis 37)

8. True (Exodus 1:8)

9. True (Exodus 3:1–3)

10. False—God inflicted ten plagues on Egypt. (Exodus 7–12)

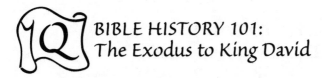

BIBLE HISTORY 101:
The Exodus to King David

Choose the correct answer to these questions about Bible history.

1. When the Israelites left Egypt during the Exodus, what did they carry on their shoulders?
   a. their belongings
   b. bowls of bitter herbs
   c. unleavened bread in kneading troughs
   d. firstborn lambs

2. Who did Moses ordain as the first high priest of Israel?
   a. Levi
   b. Joshua
   c. Abihu
   d. Aaron

3. What was the first city destroyed in the conquest of Canaan?
   a. Gilgal
   b. Jericho
   c. Ai
   d. Hebron

4. Who was the first king of Israel?
   a. Moses
   b. Saul
   c. David
   d. Solomon

5. What city was occupied by Jebusites before it was captured and became the City of David?
   a. Bethlehem
   b. Nazareth
   c. Jerusalem
   d. Hebron

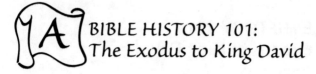

BIBLE HISTORY 101:
The Exodus to King David

1.   c. unleavened bread in kneading troughs (Exodus 12:34)

2.   d. Aaron (Leviticus 8:1–12)

3.   b. Jericho (Joshua 5, 6)

4.   b. Saul (1 Samuel 9, 10)

5.   c. Jerusalem (2 Samuel 5:6–10)

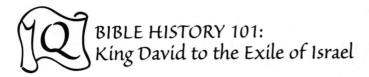

BIBLE HISTORY 101:
King David to the Exile of Israel

Fill in the blanks in these quotes about lots more key events in Bible history. (If there are two blanks in a quote, both missing words are the same.)

1. "That night the word of the Lord came to _____, saying: 'Go and tell my servant David, "The Lord declares to you that the Lord himself will establish a house for you."'"

2. "Zadok the priest took the horn of oil from the sacred tent and anointed _____. Then they sounded the trumpet and all the people shouted, 'Long live King _____!'"

3. "In the eleventh year in the month of Bul, the eighth month, the temple was finished in all its details according to its specifications. He had spent _____ years building it."

4. "When all the Israelites heard that _____ had returned, they sent and called him to the assembly and made him king over all Israel. Only the tribe of Judah remained loyal to the house of David."

5. "As they were walking along and talking together, suddenly a chariot of fire and horses of fire appeared and separated the two of them, and _____ went up to heaven in a whirlwind."

6. "In the ninth year of Hoshea, the king of _____ captured Samaria and deported the Israelites to _____."

BIBLE HISTORY 101:
King David to the Exile of Israel

1. Nathan (2 Samuel 7:4, 5, 11)

2. Solomon (1 Kings 1:39)

3. seven (1 Kings 6:38)

4. Jeroboam (1 Kings 12:20)

5. Elijah (2 Kings 2:11)

6. Assyria (2 Kings 17:6)

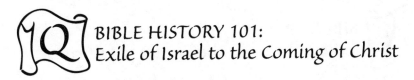

BIBLE HISTORY 101:
Exile of Israel to the Coming of Christ

Are the following statements about lots more key events in Bible history true or false? For extra credit, correct the false statements.

1. King Hezekiah prayed and asked God to deliver Jerusalem from the Assyrian commander Sennacherib.

2. During the reign of King Manasseh, the Book of the Law was found and the Passover was celebrated.

3. Nebuchadnezzar, who destroyed Jerusalem and sent Judah into exile, was the king of Persia.

4. Daniel was among the young men from Israel's royal family and nobility who were taken into exile.

5. The people began returning to Israel during the reign of Cyrus, king of Persia.

6. Nehemiah organized the rebuilding of the temple of the Lord.

7. Before Nehemiah went back to Jerusalem, he was a baker for Artaxerxes, king of Persia.

8. Esther became queen of Persia because the original queen would not dance for the king and his drunken friends.

9. Esther and her uncle Haman foiled Mordecai's plot to destroy the Jews.

10. John the Baptist was the last prophet before the coming of the Messiah.

BIBLE HISTORY 101:
Exile of Israel to the Coming of Christ

1.   True (2 Kings 19:16, 19)

2.   False—This happened during Josiah's reign. (2 Chronicles 34, 35)

3.   False—Nebuchadnezzar was a Babylonian. (2 Kings 25:8, 9, 21)

4.   True (Daniel 1:1–6)

5.   True (Ezra 10)

6.   False—Zerubbabel is credited with rebuilding the temple. (Ezra 3:8)

7.   False—He was a cupbearer. (Nehemiah 1:11)

8.   True (Esther 1)

9.   False—Esther and her uncle Mordecai foiled Haman's plot to kill the Jews. (Esther 5–8)

10. True (Matthew 3:1)

 FAKE BOOKS

In each of the following sets, only three of the four names listed are actually books of the Bible. Can you figure out which is the fake book?

1. Luke, Thomas, James, Matthew

2. 1 Timothy, 2 John, 3 Peter, 3 John

3. Ephesians, Temptations, Lamentations, Colossians

4. Job, Jude, Nod, Joel

5. Jeremiah, Isaiah, Hosea, Josiah

6. Hezekiah, Obadiah, Zephaniah, Zechariah

7. Ezra, Enoch, Esther, Ezekiel

8. Daniel, Barnabas, Amos, Jonah

9. 2 Samuel, 2 Kings, 2 Isaiah, 2 Chronicles

10. Revolutions, Deuteronomy, Romans, Exodus

A FAKE BOOKS

1. Thomas

2. 3 Peter

3. Temptations

4. Nod

5. Josiah

6. Hezekiah

7. Enoch

8. Barnabas

9. 2 Isaiah

10. Revolutions

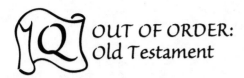

OUT OF ORDER:
Old Testament

For each of the following sets, arrange the four Old Testament books in the order they appear in the Bible.

1. Leviticus, Genesis, 1 Kings, Exodus

2. Lamentations, Isaiah, Jeremiah, 2 Chronicles

3. Nahum, Jonah, Habakkuk, Micah

4. 2 Kings, 1 Chronicles, Numbers, Song of Songs

5. Psalms, Ecclesiastes, Job, Proverbs

6. Haggai, Zephaniah, Malachi, Zechariah

7. Joel, Hosea, Daniel, Ezekiel

8. Esther, Nehemiah, Job, Ezra

9. Judges, 1 Samuel, Deuteronomy, Joshua

10. Amos, 2 Samuel, Proverbs, Ruth

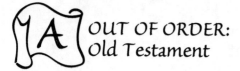

A OUT OF ORDER:
Old Testament

1. Genesis, Exodus, Leviticus, 1 Kings

2. 2 Chronicles, Isaiah, Jeremiah, Lamentations

3. Jonah, Micah, Nahum, Habakkuk

4. Numbers, 2 Kings, 1 Chronicles, Song of Songs

5. Job, Psalms, Proverbs, Ecclesiastes

6. Zephaniah, Haggai, Zechariah, Malachi

7. Ezekiel, Daniel, Hosea, Joel

8. Ezra, Nehemiah, Esther, Job

9. Deuteronomy, Joshua, Judges, 1 Samuel

10. Ruth, 2 Samuel, Proverbs, Amos

OUT OF ORDER:
New Testament

For each of the following sets, arrange the four New Testament books in the order they appear in the Bible.

1. Luke, Matthew, John, Mark

2. Acts, 1 Corinthians, John, Romans

3. Philemon, James, 1 Peter, Hebrews

4. 1 Peter, 1 Corinthians, 1 John, 1 Thessalonians

5. Ephesians, Colossians, Galatians, Philippians

6. 2 Timothy, 2 John, 2 Corinthians, Titus

7. Jude, Revelation, James, Philemon

8. 3 John, Ephesians, Hebrews, Titus

9. James, Philemon, Philippians, Romans

10. Hebrews, Colossians, Jude, Acts

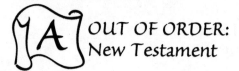

A OUT OF ORDER:
New Testament

1.   Matthew, Mark, Luke, John

2.   John, Acts, Romans, 1 Corinthians

3.   Philemon, Hebrews, James, 1 Peter

4.   1 Corinthians, 1 Thessalonians, 1 Peter, 1 John

5.   Galatians, Ephesians, Philippians, Colossians

6.   2 Corinthians, 2 Timothy, Titus, 2 John

7.   Philemon, James, Jude, Revelation

8.   Ephesians, Titus, Hebrews, 3 John

9.   Romans, Philippians, Philemon, James

10. Acts, Colossians, Hebrews, Jude

III

THE LAY
OF THE
LAND

BUILDING PROJECTS

Test your knowledge of Biblical engineering:

1. Who is "the stone the builders rejected"?
   a. Jesus
   b. Peter
   c. John the Baptist
   d. Solomon

2. Which prophet saw the Lord standing with a plumb line?
   a. Isaiah
   b. Hosea
   c. Amos
   d. Andy

3. Jesus said that the man who listens to his teachings is like the wise man who builds his house on what?
   a. rock
   b. sand
   c. clay
   d. stilts

4. Who built the first temple for the nation of Israel?
   a. David
   b. Solomon
   c. Moses
   d. Nehemiah

5. According to Peter, what kinds of stones are being built into a spiritual house?
   a. rolling stones
   b. smooth stones
   c. precious stones
   d. living stones

BUILDING PROJECTS

1. a. Jesus (Luke 20:17)

2. c. Amos (Amos 7:7–10)

3. a. rock (Matthew 7:24)

4. b. Solomon (2 Samuel 7:5)

5. d. living stones (1 Peter 2:5)

 CITY LIFE

Identify each Biblical city described in these statements.

1. In this city, Lazarus was raised from the dead, Mary anointed the feet of Jesus, and Jesus blessed his disciples just before his ascension.

2. In this city, Jesus turned water into wine and also healed a nobleman's son. In addition, this city was the home of his disciple Nathanael.

3. Elisha visited a sick king in this city. King Ahaz copied the design of an altar in this city and built one like it in Jerusalem. Paul was traveling to this city when he was converted.

4. In this city, Apollos was instructed by Aquila and Priscilla, and Paul met some of John the Baptist's disciples. Also in this city, there was a book-burning ceremony and a confrontation with worshipers of Diana.

5. Samson was imprisoned in this city after being betrayed by Delilah. This was a Philistine city. Also in this city, Philip met the Ethiopian eunuch and later baptized him.

6. In this city, Abraham built an altar to God, and David was anointed king over all of Israel. Sarah, Abraham, Isaac, and Jacob were all buried here.

7. Rachel was buried in this city, and Boaz and Ruth lived there. This city is also where David was born and anointed.

8. Philip, Andrew, and Peter lived in this city, which Jesus rebuked for its unbelief. In this city, Jesus healed a blind man.

 CITY LIFE

1. Bethany (John 11; John 12:1–11; Luke 24:50)

2. Cana (John 2:1–11; John 4:46–54; John 21:2)

3. Damascus (2 Kings 8:7; 2 Kings 16:10; Acts 9:2)

4. Ephesus (Acts 18:24–26; Acts 19:18–41; Acts 19:18–41)

5. Gaza (Judges 16:1–3; Judges 16:21; Acts 8:26–38)

6. Hebron (Genesis 13:18; 2 Samuel 5:1–5; Genesis 23:19, 25:8, 35:28, 50)

7. Bethlehem (Genesis 35:15–18; Ruth 4:11; 1 Samuel 16:4–13)

8. Bethsaida (John 1:44; Luke 10:13; Mark 8:22–26)

 MORE CITY LIFE

Identify each Biblical city described in these statements.

1. Rahab the harlot lived in this city, which was tightly shut up because of the Israelites. Also in this city, Jesus healed a blind man named Bartimaeus.

2. In this city, Jonah attempted to flee from God's command, Peter raised Dorcas from the dead, and Peter received a vision about clean and unclean food.

3. In this city, Jacob and Laban parted, eleven tribes declared war on Benjamin, and Samuel gathered Israel for prayer.

4. In this city, angels announced Jesus' birth to Mary and Joseph, and Jesus grew into manhood. Also in this city, Jesus was rejected because "only in his hometown and in his own house is a prophet without honor."

5. Samuel's parents lived in this city, and Samuel was buried there. Also in this city, Israel gathered to demand a king.

6. In this city, Paul preached for two years while under house arrest, and Onesiphorus searched hard for Paul until he found him. People from this city were also present at Pentecost.

7. Jesus stayed in this city during much of his early ministry, and he also healed the centurion's servant and Peter's mother-in-law there.

8. Priscilla and Aquila lived in this city, where God appeared to Paul in a vision, encouraging him to keep on speaking. The church in this city received two of Paul's letters.

MORE CITY LIFE

1. Jericho (Joshua 2; Joshua 6; Luke 18:34)

2. Joppa (Jonah 1:3; Acts 9:36–41; Acts 9:43)

3. Mizpah (Genesis 31:49; Judges 21:1–8; 1 Samuel 7: 5–7)

4. Nazareth (Luke 1:26; Matthew 1:19, 20; Luke 2:39, 40;
    Matthew 13:57)

5. Ramah (1 Samuel 1:19; 1 Samuel 8:4; 1 Samuel 25:1)

6. Rome (Acts 29:30; Acts 2:10; 2 Timothy 1:17)

7. Capernaum (Matthew 4:13, 9:1, 8:5–13, 8:14, 15)

8. Corinth (Acts 18:1, 2; Acts 18:9, 1 Corinthians 1:1; 2
    Corinthians 1:1)

EVEN MORE CITY LIFE

Identify each Biblical city described in these statements.

1. Abraham worshiped in this city when he came into Palestine. Also in this city, Jacob dreamed about a ladder coming down from heaven, and Jeroboam set up golden calf images.

2. Cornelius lived in this city. Also in this city, God struck down Herod Agrippa I, and Paul spoke to Felix about Jesus.

3. Israel stopped here first after crossing the Jordan river. In this city, Saul was publicly proclaimed king, and Elisha purified a pot of stew.

4. This was a Roman colony and leading city in Macedonia. In this city, Lydia believed in the gospel, and she and her household were baptized. Also in this city, Paul cast out an evil spirit from a slave girl.

5. In this city, Jacob buried his household's false gods, Joseph's bones were buried, and Joshua gave his farewell address.

6. In this city, Paul had a vision of a man begging him to come to Macedonia. Also in this city, Eutychus was raised from the dead. Paul left his cloak with Carpus in this city.

7. King Omri built this city as the capital of the Northern Kingdom (Israel). Also in this city, Ahab died beside a pool. Philip proclaimed Christ in this city.

8. In this city, Joshua divided up the promised land among the tribes, Hannah prayed for a son, and the surviving warriors from the tribe of Benjamin found wives.

EVEN MORE CITY LIFE

1. Bethel (Genesis 12:8, 13:3, 4; Genesis 28:11–19; 1 Kings 12:26–29)

2. Caesarea (Acts 10:1–18; Acts 12:19–23; Acts 24:25)

3. Gilgal (Joshua 4:19; 1 Samuel 11:14; 2 Kings 4:38–41)

4. Philippi (Acts 16:12; Acts 16:14, 15; Acts 16:16–18)

5. Shechem (Genesis 35:4; Joshua 24:32; Joshua 24:1)

6. Troas (Acts 16:6–10; Acts 20:7–12; 2 Timothy 4:13)

7. Samaria (1 Kings 16:24; 1 Kings 22:37, 38; Acts 8:5–8)

8. Shiloh (Joshua 18:2–10; 1 Samuel 1; Judges 21:16–23)

THE BIBLE'S BIG APPLE

Choose the correct answer to these questions about Jerusalem.

1. Who lived in Jerusalem before David captured it?
    a. Jerusalemites
    b. Flashlites
    c. Jebusites
    d. Hittites

2. Which of David's sons rebelled against him, temporarily occupied Jerusalem, and lay with David's concubines?
    a. Solomon
    b. Adonijah
    c. Nathan
    d. Absalom

3. During whose reign was Jerusalem burned by the Babylonians?
    a. Zedekiah
    b. Hezekiah
    c. Jumpahiah
    d. Mezakiah

4. Where will the "new Jerusalem" come from?
    a. the ashes of the old
    b. rise out of the water
    c. be built by the Church
    d. come down from heaven

5. When Jesus entered Jerusalem the week of his crucifixion, the people took palm branches and shouted what?
    a. Hallelujah!
    b. Amen, Amen!
    c. Hosanna!
    d. Crucify him!

THE BIBLE'S BIG APPLE

1. c. Jebusites (2 Samuel 5:6–12)

2. d. Absalom (2 Samuel 16:15–22)

3. a. Zedekiah (2 Kings 25)

4. d. come down from heaven (Revelation 21:2)

5. c. Hosanna! (Mark 11)

THE WRITING'S ON THE WALL

Choose the correct answer to these questions about Bible walls.

1. What city's walls fell when trumpets sounded and people shouted?
   a. Jerusalem
   b. Babel
   c. Jericho
   d. Ai

2. What was thrown to Joab over the wall of Abel Beth Maacah?
   a. a baby
   b. a millstone
   c. food
   d. the head of Sheba

3. What did the desperate king of Moab do on the wall of his city as Israel battled against him?
   a. He sacrificed his son.
   b. He fell on his sword.
   c. He jumped off.
   d. He cried out to Israel's God.

4. What horrible story did King Joram hear as he walked along the wall of his besieged city?
   a. His sons were assassinated.
   b. Women were eating their children.
   c. Leprosy broke out on his wife's face.
   d. Dogs were eating the dead.

5. Whose body was fastened to the wall of Beth Shan?
   a. Goliath
   b. Haman
   c. Saul
   d. Absalom

THE WRITING'S ON THE WALL

1. c. Jericho (Joshua 6:20)

2. d. the head of Sheba (2 Samuel 20:22)

3. a. He sacrificed his son. (2 Kings 3:27)

4. b. Women were eating their children. (2 Kings 6:28, 29)

5. c. Saul (1 Samuel 31:10)

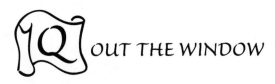 OUT THE WINDOW

Identify the person described in each of the following windows stories from the Bible.

1. She painted her eyes, arranged her hair, and looked out a window at Jehu. Minutes later, she was thrown from the window to her death.

2. He went to sleep during one of Paul's sermons and fell out the window.

3. Israelite spies escaped out this person's window using a scarlet cord.

4. She watched through her window as David leaped and danced before the Lord, and she despised him in her heart.

5. He ordered King Jehoash to open the east window and shoot "the Lord's arrow of victory."

6. He went upstairs where the windows opened toward Jerusalem and prayed three times a day.

7. He slipped through the hands of the governor of Damascus by being lowered in a basket through a window in the wall.

8. He sent a dove out a window to look for dry land.

9. He looked out a window and saw Isaac caressing his wife, Rebekah.

10. His wife let him down through a window in order to escape King Saul.

OUT THE WINDOW

1. Jezebel (2 Kings 9:30–33)

2. Eutychus (Acts 20:9)

3. Rahab (Joshua 2:18)

4. Michal (2 Samuel 6:16)

5. Elisha (2 Kings 13:17)

6. Daniel (Daniel 6:10)

7. Paul (2 Corinthians 11:32)

8. Noah (Genesis 8:6–12)

9. Abimelech (Genesis 26:8)

10. David (1 Samuel 19:12)

 MAJOR MOUNTAINS

Identify the famous Bible mountains associated with each of the following events. (Choices: Horeb, Tabor, Moriah, Zion, Olives, Ararat, Everest, Hor, Seir, Sinai, Carmel)

1. Moses received the Ten Commandments.

2. Noah's ark came to rest.

3. Aaron gave his priestly garments to his son and died.

4. Jesus and his disciples went here after the Last Supper.

5. Elijah challenged the prophets of Baal.

6. The sons of Esau were given an inheritance.

7. God spoke to Moses from the burning bush.

8. Deborah defeated the forces of Sisera.

9. Abraham offered to sacrifice his son, Isaac.

10. David captured the fortress and made it his city.

MAJOR MOUNTAINS

1. Sinai (Exodus 19)

2. Ararat (Genesis 8:4)

3. Hor (Numbers 20:27, 28)

4. Olives (Matthew 26:30)

5. Carmel (1 Kings 18:19)

6. Seir (Joshua 24:4)

7. Horeb (Exodus 3:2, 3)

8. Tabor (Judges 4:6–16)

9. Moriah (Genesis 22:2)

10. Zion (2 Samuel 5:7)

 WATER WAYS

On the left is a list of famous bodies of water, and on the right, descriptions of them or Biblical events associated with them. Can you match the waterway with the description or event?

1. ___ Jordan

2. ___ Tigris and Euphrates

3. ___ Salt Sea

4. ___ Red Sea

5. ___ Sea of Galilee

6. ___ Nile

7. ___ Arnon

8. ___ Jabbok

9. ___ Kishon

10. ___ Kebar

a. also called the Sea of Arabah

b. Jesus called Peter and Andrew

c. Israel's boundary with Moab

d. Sisera's army is defeated

e. parted by Joshua

f. turned to blood by Moses

g. Ezekiel saw a vision

h. Jacob wrestled with an angel

i. parted by Moses

j. flowed in the garden of Eden

WATER WAYS

1. e. parted by Joshua (Joshua 3:13–17)

2. j. flowed in the garden of Eden (Genesis 2:14)

3. a. also called the Sea of Arabah (Joshua 3:16)

4. i. parted by Moses (Exodus 14:21)

5. b. Jesus called Peter and Andrew (Mark 1:16)

6. f. turned to blood by Moses (Exodus 7:17–25)

7. c. Israel's boundary with Moab (Numbers 21:13)

8. h. Jacob wrestled with an angel (Genesis 32)

9. d. Sisera's army is defeated (Judges 5:21)

10. g. Ezekiel saw a vision (Ezekiel 1:1)

 NEVER FORGET

On the left is a list of memorials, and on the right, the things they memorialize. Can you match the memorial with the memorialized?

1. ___ Rainbow

2. ___ Passover

3. ___ bronze censers

4. ___ Sabbath

5. ___ twelve stones

6. ___ manna in the ark

7. ___ Purim

8. ___ Feast of Tabernacles

9. ___ two stones on the ephod

10. ___ Last Supper

a. God's provision in the desert

b. Israel's deliverance from Egypt

c. salvation from wicked Haman

d. the body and blood of Christ

e. when the blood of a lamb saved people from judgment

f. completed creation

g. God would never destroy the world with a flood

h. only Aaron's descendants may offer incense

i. Israel's crossing the Jordan with God's power

j. remember the sons of Israel before the Lord

NEVER FORGET

1. g. God would never again destroy the world with a flood (Genesis 9:13–16)

2. e. when the blood of a lamb saved people from judgment (Exodus 12:11–14)

3. h. only Aaron's descendants may offer incense (Numbers 16:39, 40)

4. f. completed creation (Deuteronomy 5:15)

5. i. Israel's crossing the Jordan with God's power (Joshua 4:7)

6. a. God's provision in the desert (Exodus 16:32)

7. c. salvation from wicked Haman (Esther 9:28)

8. b. Israel's deliverance from Egypt (Leviticus 23:39–43)

9. j. remember the sons of Israel before the Lord (Exodus 28:9–12)

10. d. the body and blood of Christ (Luke 22:19)

IV

PERSONALITY PARADE

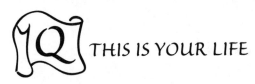 THIS IS YOUR LIFE

Choose the statement that was actually true of each person's life.

1. Eve
   a. was made from her husband's thighbone.
   b. had a son named Seth.
   c. starred in *All About Eve*.
   d. was turned into a pillar of salt.

2. Abraham
   a. signed the Emancipation Proclamation.
   b. made an axhead float.
   c. made a strawberry float.
   d. met the Lord at Mamre.

3. Jacob
   a. tricked his father into sacrificing him on a mountain.
   b. tricked his father into blessing him.
   c. tricked Laban into giving him his sheep.
   d. tricked Esau into eating stew.

4. Moses
   a. had two sons, Jacob and Esau.
   b. had a sprouting staff.
   c. parted the Jordan River.
   d. murdered an Egyptian.

5. Ruth
   a. became Boaz's wife.
   b. became an advice columnist.
   c. became a queen of Israel.
   d. became the mother of Solomon.

THIS IS YOUR LIFE

1. b. had a son named Seth. (Genesis 4:25)

2. d. met the Lord at Mamre. (Genesis 18:1)

3. b. tricked his father into blessing him. (Genesis 27)

4. d. murdered an Egyptian. (Exodus 2:12)

5. a. became Boaz's wife. (Ruth 4:13)

THIS IS NOT YOUR LIFE

Choose the statement that is not true about each person's life.

1. Isaiah
    a. was the son of Amoz.
    b. never married.
    c. prophesied during Uzziah's reign.
    d. prophesied during Ahaz's reign.

2. Jeremiah
    a. had a secretary named Baruch.
    b. was thrown into a well.
    c. began prophesying during Josiah's reign.
    d. once ran around naked.

3. David
    a. was the son of Saul.
    b. worked as a shepherd.
    c. married Bathsheba.
    d. killed Goliath.

4. Peter
    a. was a fisherman.
    b. was the brother of Andrew.
    c. walked on water.
    d. was known as "the disciple Jesus loved."

5. Paul
    a. was a Pharisee.
    b. was converted on the road to Emmaus.
    c. was born in Tarsus.
    d. was of the tribe of Benjamin.

THIS IS NOT YOUR LIFE

1. b. never married. (Isaiah 8:3)

2. d. once ran around naked. (Isaiah 20:2)

3. a. was the son of Saul. (1 Samuel 16:19)

4. d. was known as "the disciple Jesus loved." (John 21:21, 24)

5. b. was converted on the road to Emmaus. (Acts 9:3)

PAUL AND THE NUMBER THREE

Can you answer these questions about Paul's life that involve the number three?

1. What disability did Paul suffer from for three days after his conversion?

2. According to Paul, what are the three enduring virtues?

3. In what city did a riot break out after Paul spoke in the synagogue for three Sabbath days?

4. In what city did Paul speak in the synagogue for three months before relocating to the lecture hall of Tyrannus?

5. How many months did Paul stay in Greece?

6. What type of disaster did Paul experience three times?

7. What kind of punishment did Paul suffer three times?

8. What did Paul plead with God three times to remove?

9. After coming ashore in Malta, in whose house did Paul stay for three days?

10. On his way to Rome, Paul met believers at the Forum of Appius and at what other town?

PAUL AND THE NUMBER THREE

1. He was blind. (Acts 9:9)

2. faith, hope, and love (1 Corinthians 13:13)

3. Thessalonica (Acts 17:1–9)

4. Ephesus (Acts 19:8)

5. three! (Acts 20:3)

6. shipwreck (2 Corinthians 11:25)

7. being beaten with rods (2 Corinthians 11:25)

8. a thorn in his flesh (2 Corinthians 12:8)

9. Publius's house (Acts 28:7)

10. Three Taverns (Acts 28:15)

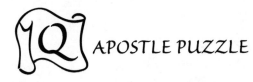

APOSTLE PUZZLE

For each of these questions, fill in the blank with the missing name of one of Jesus' apostles.

1. _____ was the brother of Andrew.

2. John was the brother of _____.

3. _____ introduced his friend Nathanael to Jesus.

4. _____ was a member of a radical political party.

5. Jesus said to _____: "I saw you while you were still under the fig tree."

6. _____ acted as treasurer for the apostles.

7. _____ was chosen by lot to join the apostles.

8. Before he became an apostle, _____ was a tax collector.

9. _____ was the son of Alphaeus.

10. _____ wanted to put his hand in the wound in Jesus' side.

APOSTLE PUZZLE

1.   Peter (John 1:40)

2.   James (Matthew 4:21)

3.   Philip (John 1:43)

4.   Simon (Matthew 10:4)

5.   Nathanael (John 1:48)

6.   Judas (John 13:29)

7.   Matthias (Acts 1:26)

8.   Matthew (Matthew 10:3)

9.   James (Matthew 10:3)

10.   Thomas (John 20:25)

 CLAIM TO FAME

Can you answer the following questions about Biblical characters with superlative qualities?

1. Who was the earliest human being?

2. Who was wiser than anyone who had come before him and anyone who would come after?

3. Who was over nine feet tall?

4. Who was so short that he had to climb a sycamore tree to see over the crowd?

5. Who was described as more humble than anyone on the face of the earth?

6. Who did Jesus describe as "the greatest among those born of women"?

7. What king of Judah was described as doing more evil than the nations the Lord had destroyed before the Israelites?

8. What king was so scared at seeing fingers writing on the wall that his face turned pale, his knees knocked together, and his legs gave way?

9. Who was so lovestruck that he agreed to work seven years for the hand of his bride-to-be?

10. Who has the longest name in the Bible?

CLAIM TO FAME

1. Adam (Genesis 2:7)

2. Solomon (1 Kings 3:12)

3. Goliath (1 Samuel 17:4)

4. Zacchaeus (Luke 19:3, 4)

5. Moses (Numbers 12:3)

6. John the Baptist (Matthew 11:11)

7. Manasseh (2 Chronicles 33:9)

8. King Belshazzar (Daniel 5:5, 6)

9. Jacob (Genesis 29:18–20)

10. Maher-shalal-hash-baz (Isaiah 8:1–4)

WOMEN'S RIGHTS (AND WRONGS)

Identify each famous Bible woman described in these statements.

1. She and her husband, Aquila, were among Paul's closest companions.

2. The circumstance surrounding her marriage were scandalous, but her son eventually became a king of Israel.

3. This well-to-do woman from Thyatira became a Christian and invited Paul and his companions to stay at her house.

4. Jesus stayed at this woman's house, but she was so distracted with dinner preparations that she never sat and listened to his teaching.

5. Because this queen's influence saved the Jews, the celebration of Purim was established.

6. This woman got her name because she would become the mother of all the living.

7. This widow found a new husband and a new country, and her great-grandson became a king of Israel.

8. She was a prophetess and a leader of Israel, and her husband's name was Lappidoth.

9. She laughed on hearing that she would have a child in her old age.

10. This woman was a servant of the church of Cenchrea, and Paul said she was a great help to many people, including him.

WOMEN'S RIGHTS (AND WRONGS)

1. Priscilla (Acts 18:18)

2. Bathsheba (1 Kings 1:28–31)

3. Lydia (Acts 16:14, 15)

4. Martha (Luke 10:38–41)

5. Esther (Esther 9)

6. Eve (Genesis 3:20)

7. Ruth (Ruth 4:13–22)

8. Deborah (Judges 4)

9. Sarah (Genesis 18:12)

10. Phoebe (Romans 16:1, 2)

MORE WOMEN'S RIGHTS (AND WRONGS)

Identify each famous Bible woman described in these statements.

1. She is one of the few prophetesses in the Bible, and she told king Josiah that he would not have to experience the disaster God was going to bring on Judah.

2. This eighty-four-year-old prophetess approached Mary and Joseph and thanked God for the infant Jesus.

3. Without the help of this lady of ill repute, Joshua's spies would have ended up in the Jericho jail.

4. This beautiful woman's job was to lay next to the aging King David and keep him warm.

5. She lost her life because her husband sold land and then lied about it to the church.

6. This sister of Aaron celebrated the destruction of Pharaoh's army by taking up a tambourine and leading the women in singing and dancing.

7. She was known for doing good and helping the poor. Peter raised her from the dead.

8. She heard these words from her future husband: "May you be blessed for your good judgment and for keeping me from bloodshed this day and from avenging myself with my own hands."

9. She was the only woman to rule over Judah.

10. She and the apostle Paul were not married, but they both called Timothy their son.

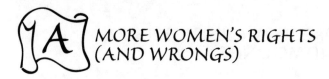

MORE WOMEN'S RIGHTS (AND WRONGS)

1. Huldah (2 Kings 22:14–20)

2. Anna (Luke 2:36–38)

3. Rahab (Joshua 2)

4. Abishag (1 Kings 1:2–4)

5. Sapphira (Acts 5)

6. Miriam (Exodus 15:20)

7. Dorcas (Acts 9:36–43)

8. Abigail (1 Samuel 25:32)

9. Athaliah (2 Kings 11)

10. Eunice (2 Timothy 1:5)

MORE WHAT'S IN A NAME?

"Sons of Thunder." (Mark 3:18)

"There is no glory in Israel." (1 Samuel 4:21)

she drew him out of the water. (Exodus 2:10)

he would save his people. (Matthew 1:21)

Place of the Skull. (Matthew 27:33)

 WHAT'S IN A NAME?

Choose the correct meaning or origin of each of these Bible names.

1. "Peter" means
   a. "the first."
   b. "the rock."
   c. "the fisherman."
   d. "the red."

2. "Immanuel" means
   a. "righteous one."
   b. "savior."
   c. "God with us."
   d. "godly."

3. "Peniel" means
   a. "face of God."
   b. "arm of God."
   c. "power of God."
   d. "pen of God."

4. "Nabal" means
   a. "friend."
   b. "foe."
   c. "fool."
   d. "Frank."

5. "Barnabas" means
   a. "Son of Light."
   b. "Son of a Gun."
   c. "Son of Encouragement."
   d. "Son of Man."

WHAT'S IN A NAME?

1. b. "the rock." (Matthew 16:18)

2. c. "God with us." (Matthew 1:23)

3. a. "face of God." (Genesis 32:31)

4. c. "fool." (1 Samuel 25:25)

5. c. "Son of Encouragement." (Acts 4:36)

 **MORE WHAT'S IN**

Choose the correct meaning or origin of

1. James and John were called "Boar
   a. "Twins."
   b. "Sons of Boan."
   c. "Brave Hearts."
   d. "Sons of Thunder."

2. Eli's daughter-in-law named her so
   a. "What an icky body!"
   b. "There is no glory in Israel."
   c. "He is a blessing from the Lord.
   d. "The Lord has remembered."

3. Pharaoh's daughter named the boy '
   a. it was a family name.
   b. he would deliver Israel.
   c. she wanted to conceal his identity
   d. she drew him out of the water.

4. The angel instructed Joseph to give h
   "Jesus" because
   a. he would save his people.
   b. he was the son of God.
   c. he was the Holy One.
   d. "Joseph Christ" didn't sound right.

5. Jesus was crucified on Golgotha, which
   a. Place of Death.
   b. Place of the Skull.
   c. Place of the Cross.
   d. Place of Tears.

1. d.

2. b.

3. d.

4. a.

5. b.

ALSO KNOWN AS . . .

Some people in the Bible were known by more than one name. Match the person with his or her "other" name.

1. ___ Saul   a. Justus

2. ___ Thomas   b. Satan

3. ___ Abraham   c. Magdalene

4. ___ Simon   d. Sarai

5. ___ Barsabbas   e. Abram

6. ___ Devil   f. Mark

7. ___ Jacob   g. Didymus

8. ___ Sarah   h. Peter

9. ___ Mary   i. Israel

10. ___ John   j. Paul

ALSO KNOWN AS ...

1. j. Paul (Acts 13:9)

2. g. Didymus (John 11:16)

3. e. Abram (Genesis 17:5)

4. h. Peter (Matthew 4:18)

5. a. Justus (Acts 1:23)

6. b. Satan (Revelation 12:9)

7. i. Israel (Genesis 35:10)

8. d. Sarai (Genesis 17:15)

9. c. Magdalene (Luke 8:2)

10. f. Mark (Acts 12:25)

 IN COMMON

What do the following pairs of people have in common with one another?

1. Sarai and Keturah

2. Moses and David

3. Naboth and Stephen

4. Lazarus and Tabitha

5. Jonah and Paul

6. Enoch and Elijah

7. Haman and Judas

8. Goliath and John the Baptist

9. Andrew and James

10. Sarah and Elizabeth

A IN COMMON

1. They both were wives of Abraham. (Genesis 11:29; 25:1)

2. They both once worked as shepherds. (Exodus 3:1; 1 Samuel 16:11)

3. They both were stoned to death. (1 Kings 21:13; Acts 7:58)

4. They both were raised from the dead. (John 11:43, 44; Acts 9:40, 41)

5. They both nearly lost their lives in a storm at sea. (Jonah 1; Acts 27)

6. Neither of the two died. (Genesis 5:24; 2 Kings 2:11)

7. They both were hanged. (Esther 7:10; Matthew 27:5)

8. They both had their heads cut off. (1 Samuel 17:51; Matthew 14:1–12)

9. They both made their living by fishing. (Matthew 4:18–22)

10. They both had sons in their old age. (Genesis 18:11; Luke 1:7)

V

THE
MAIN
MAN

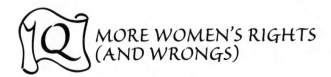

MORE WOMEN'S RIGHTS (AND WRONGS)

Identify each famous Bible woman described in these statements.

1. She is one of the few prophetesses in the Bible, and she told king Josiah that he would not have to experience the disaster God was going to bring on Judah.

2. This eighty-four-year-old prophetess approached Mary and Joseph and thanked God for the infant Jesus.

3. Without the help of this lady of ill repute, Joshua's spies would have ended up in the Jericho jail.

4. This beautiful woman's job was to lay next to the aging King David and keep him warm.

5. She lost her life because her husband sold land and then lied about it to the church.

6. This sister of Aaron celebrated the destruction of Pharaoh's army by taking up a tambourine and leading the women in singing and dancing.

7. She was known for doing good and helping the poor. Peter raised her from the dead.

8. She heard these words from her future husband: "May you be blessed for your good judgment and for keeping me from bloodshed this day and from avenging myself with my own hands."

9. She was the only woman to rule over Judah.

10. She and the apostle Paul were not married, but they both called Timothy their son.

MORE WOMEN'S RIGHTS (AND WRONGS)

1. Huldah (2 Kings 22:14–20)

2. Anna (Luke 2:36–38)

3. Rahab (Joshua 2)

4. Abishag (1 Kings 1:2–4)

5. Sapphira (Acts 5)

6. Miriam (Exodus 15:20)

7. Dorcas (Acts 9:36–43)

8. Abigail (1 Samuel 25:32)

9. Athaliah (2 Kings 11)

10. Eunice (2 Timothy 1:5)

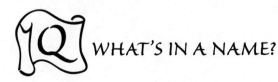 WHAT'S IN A NAME?

Choose the correct meaning or origin of each of these Bible names.

1. "Peter" means
   a. "the first."
   b. "the rock."
   c. "the fisherman."
   d. "the red."

2. "Immanuel" means
   a. "righteous one."
   b. "savior."
   c. "God with us."
   d. "godly."

3. "Peniel" means
   a. "face of God."
   b. "arm of God."
   c. "power of God."
   d. "pen of God."

4. "Nabal" means
   a. "friend."
   b. "foe."
   c. "fool."
   d. "Frank."

5. "Barnabas" means
   a. "Son of Light."
   b. "Son of a Gun."
   c. "Son of Encouragement."
   d. "Son of Man."

WHAT'S IN A NAME?

1. b. "the rock." (Matthew 16:18)

2. c. "God with us." (Matthew 1:23)

3. a. "face of God." (Genesis 32:31)

4. c. "fool." (1 Samuel 25:25)

5. c. "Son of Encouragement." (Acts 4:36)

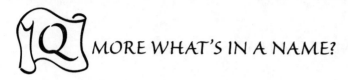

MORE WHAT'S IN A NAME?

Choose the correct meaning or origin of each of these Bible names.

1. James and John were called "Boanerges," which means
    a. "Twins."
    b. "Sons of Boan."
    c. "Brave Hearts."
    d. "Sons of Thunder."

2. Eli's daughter-in-law named her son "Ichabod," saying:
    a. "What an icky body!"
    b. "There is no glory in Israel."
    c. "He is a blessing from the Lord."
    d. "The Lord has remembered."

3. Pharaoh's daughter named the boy "Moses" because
    a. it was a family name.
    b. he would deliver Israel.
    c. she wanted to conceal his identity.
    d. she drew him out of the water.

4. The angel instructed Joseph to give his son the name
    "Jesus" because
    a. he would save his people.
    b. he was the son of God.
    c. he was the Holy One.
    d. "Joseph Christ" didn't sound right.

5. Jesus was crucified on Golgotha, which means:
    a. Place of Death.
    b. Place of the Skull.
    c. Place of the Cross.
    d. Place of Tears.

MORE WHAT'S IN A NAME?

1. d. "Sons of Thunder." (Mark 3:18)

2. b. "There is no glory in Israel." (1 Samuel 4:21)

3. d. she drew him out of the water. (Exodus 2:10)

4. a. he would save his people. (Matthew 1:21)

5. b. Place of the Skull. (Matthew 27:33)

ALSO KNOWN AS...

Some people in the Bible were known by more than one name. Match the person with his or her "other" name.

1. ___ Saul   a. Justus

2. ___ Thomas   b. Satan

3. ___ Abraham   c. Magdalene

4. ___ Simon   d. Sarai

5. ___ Barsabbas   e. Abram

6. ___ Devil   f. Mark

7. ___ Jacob   g. Didymus

8. ___ Sarah   h. Peter

9. ___ Mary   i. Israel

10. ___ John   j. Paul

ALSO KNOWN AS ...

1. j. Paul (Acts 13:9)

2. g. Didymus (John 11:16)

3. e. Abram (Genesis 17:5)

4. h. Peter (Matthew 4:18)

5. a. Justus (Acts 1:23)

6. b. Satan (Revelation 12:9)

7. i. Israel (Genesis 35:10)

8. d. Sarai (Genesis 17:15)

9. c. Magdalene (Luke 8:2)

10. f. Mark (Acts 12:25)

IN COMMON

What do the following pairs of people have in common with one another?

1. Sarai and Keturah

2. Moses and David

3. Naboth and Stephen

4. Lazarus and Tabitha

5. Jonah and Paul

6. Enoch and Elijah

7. Haman and Judas

8. Goliath and John the Baptist

9. Andrew and James

10. Sarah and Elizabeth

IN COMMON

1.   They both were wives of Abraham. (Genesis 11:29; 25:1)

2.   They both once worked as shepherds. (Exodus 3:1;
      1 Samuel 16:11)

3.   They both were stoned to death. (1 Kings 21:13; Acts 7:58)

4.   They both were raised from the dead. (John 11:43, 44;
      Acts 9:40, 41)

5.   They both nearly lost their lives in a storm at sea. (Jonah 1;
      Acts 27)

6.   Neither of the two died. (Genesis 5:24; 2 Kings 2:11)

7.   They both were hanged. (Esther 7:10; Matthew 27:5)

8.   They both had their heads cut off. (1 Samuel 17:51;
      Matthew 14:1–12)

9.   They both made their living by fishing. (Matthew 4:18–22)

10.   They both had sons in their old age. (Genesis 18:11; Luke 1:7)

V

THE
MAIN
MAN

 THE FIRST NOËL

Test your knowledge of Jesus' birth with these questions.

1. Who was the governor of Syria at the time of Jesus' birth?

2. What event brought Mary and Joseph to Bethlehem?

3. Who was Caesar at the time of Jesus' birth?

4. Which Old Testament king was Joseph a descendant of?

5. Where did the angel appear to Joseph?

6. How long did Mary stay with Elizabeth?

7. What happened to Elizabeth when she heard Mary's greeting?

8. What other famous Bible figure was born in Bethlehem?

9. What did the angels say (to the shepherds) would be the sign that the Savior had been born?

10. How much younger than John the Baptist was Jesus?

THE FIRST NOËL

1. Quirinius (Luke 2:2)

2. a census (Luke 2:2)

3. Augustus (Luke 2:1)

4. David (Luke 1:27)

5. in a dream (Luke 1:20)

6. three months (Luke 1:56)

7. The baby leaped in her womb, and she was filled with the Holy Spirit. (Luke 1:41)

8. David (Luke 2:4, 1 Samuel 17:12)

9. They would find a baby wrapped in cloths and lying in a manger. (Luke 2:12)

10. six months—Elizabeth was in her sixth month of pregnancy when the angel visited Mary (Luke 1:26)

GET IN LINE:
The Life of Jesus

Arrange these events from the life of Jesus in their correct historical order.

1. ___

2. ___

3. ___

4. ___

5. ___

6. ___

7. ___

8. ___

9. ___

10. ___

a. Peter acknowledges that Jesus is the Christ.

b. John the apostle receives a vision on the island of Patmos concerning seven churches.

c. Paul preaches to philosophers in Athens.

d. The Holy Spirit descends on Jesus like a dove.

e. Paul and Barnabas are sent out by the church.

f. Jesus appears to two disciples on the road to Emmaus.

g. Peter heals a crippled beggar outside the temple.

h. The Holy Spirit is poured out at Pentecost.

i. Judas commits suicide.

j. Peter denies Jesus three times.

GET IN LINE:
The Life of Jesus

1. d. The Holy Spirit descends on Jesus like a dove. (Matthew 3)

2. a. Peter acknowledges that Jesus is the Christ. (Matthew 11)

3. j. Peter denies Jesus three times. (John 18)

4. f. Jesus appears to two disciples on the road to Emmaus. (Luke 24)

5. i. Judas commits suicide. (Acts 1)

6. h. The Holy Spirit is poured out at Pentecost. (Acts 2)

7. g. Peter heals a crippled beggar outside the temple. (Acts 3)

8. e. Paul and Barnabas are sent out by the church. (Acts 13)

9. c. Paul preaches to philosophers in Athens. (Acts 17)

10. b. John the apostle receives a vision on the island of Patmos concerning seven churches. (Revelation 1)

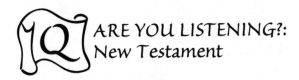 ARE YOU LISTENING?:
New Testament

To whom did Jesus address the following questions?

1. "Can you drink the cup I drink or be baptized with the baptism I am baptized with?"

2. "Dear woman, why do you involve me? My time has not yet come."

3. "Why do you call me good? No one is good—except God alone."

4. "But what about you? Who do you say I am?"

5. "I have spoken to you of earthly things and you have not believed me; how then will you believe if I speak of heavenly things?"

6. "Will you give me a drink?"

7. "Do you want to be well?"

8. "How many loaves do you have?"

9. "And whoever lives and believes in me will never die. Do you believe this?"

10. "How can you say, 'Show us the Father'? Don't you believe that I am in the Father, and that the Father is in me?"

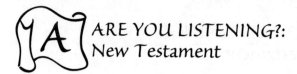

ARE YOU LISTENING?: New Testament

1. James and John (Mark 10:38)

2. Mary, the mother of Jesus (John 2:4)

3. the rich young ruler (Mark 10:18)

4. Peter (Mark 8:29)

5. Nicodemus (John 3:12)

6. the Samaritan woman (John 4:7)

7. the man by the pool of Bethesda (John 5:6)

8. the disciples (Matthew 15:34)

9. Martha (John 11:26)

10. Philip (John 14:9, 10)

JESUS AND THE NUMBER THREE

Answer the following questions about Jesus' life that involve the number three.

1. What three gifts did the Magi present to the infant Jesus?

2. Who looked for Jesus for three days in Jerusalem?

3. Jesus spent the most time with which three apostles?

4. Who were the other two people who appeared with Jesus when he was transfigured?

5. Who denied Jesus three times?

6. What question did Jesus ask Peter three times?

7. In the garden of Gethsemane, Jesus returned to his disciples three times and found them doing what?

8. According to the gospel of John, who were the three Marys who stood near the cross at Jesus' crucifixion?

9. What happened to Jesus on the third day after his death?

10. Who are the three members of the Trinity?

JESUS AND THE NUMBER THREE

1. gold, incense (frankincense), myrrh (Matthew 2:11)

2. his parents (Luke 2:46)

3. Peter, James, and John (Mark 14:33) (Matthew 17:1)

4. Moses and Elijah (Matthew 17:3)

5. Peter (John 13:38)

6. "Do you love me?" (John 21:15–17)

7. sleeping (Matthew 26:36–46)

8. Mary, Jesus' mother; Mary the wife of Clopas; and Mary Magdalene (John 19:25)

9. He was resurrected. (Matthew 28)

10. Father, Son, and Holy Spirit (Matthew 28:19)

 IN HIS NAME

Fill in the blanks to complete these names and titles for Jesus. (The first letter of each missing word has been provided for you.)

1. Bright Morning S_____

2. G_____ Shepherd

3. Root of D_____

4. Son of G_____

5. Son of M_____

6. Son of D_____

7. The A_____ and the O_____

8. I_____

9. S_____

10. Lord of L_____

IN HIS NAME

1. Bright Morning Star (Revelation 22:16)

2. Good Shepherd (John 10:11)

3. Root of David (Revelation 22:16)

4. Son of God (Luke 1:35)

5. Son of Man (Matthew 18:11)

6. Son of David (Matthew 15:22)

7. The Alpha and the Omega (Revelation 1:8)

8. Immanuel (Matthew 1:23)

9. Savior (Luke 1:47)

10. Lord of Lords (Revelation 19:16)

MISSING ANIMALS

In these words of Jesus, fill in the blanks with the missing animal (or bug or bird).

1. "Watch out for false prophets. They come to you in sheep's clothing, but inwardly they are ferocious _____."

2. "I tell you the truth, I am the gate for the _____."

3. "So don't be afraid; you are worth more than many _____."

4. "It is not right to take the children's bread and toss it to their _____."

5. "_____ have holes and birds of the air have their nests, but the Son of Man has no place to lay his head."

6. "It is easier for a _____ to go through the eye of a needle than for a rich man to enter the kingdom of God."

7. "He will put the _____ on his right and the _____ on his left."

8. "If one of you had an _____ that falls into the well on a Sabbath day, will you not immediately pull him out?"

9. "He longed to fill his stomach with pods that the _____ were eating, but no one gave him anything."

10. "You blind guides. You strain out a _____ but swallow a camel."

MISSING ANIMALS

1. wolves (Matthew 7:15)

2. sheep (John 10:7)

3. sparrows (Matthew 10:31)

4. dogs (Matthew 15:26)

5. Foxes (Matthew 8:20)

6. camel (Matthew 19:24)

7. sheep, goats (Matthew 25:33)

8. ox (Luke 14:5)

9. pigs (Luke 15:16)

10. gnat (Matthew 23:24)

THE MOST FAMOUS FINISH

The following statements describe a person associated with the death and resurrection of Jesus. For each, identify the person. (Choices: Elijah, Herod, Peter, Thomas, Nicodemus, Joseph, Pilate, Barabbas, Caiaphas, Simon, Judas)

1. He betrayed Jesus.

2. He was the high priest at the time.

3. He was a criminal released in Jesus' place.

4. He was the governor at the time.

5. Jesus was buried in his tomb.

6. The spectators thought Jesus was crying out for this person.

7. He helped Jesus carry the cross.

8. He was the first apostle to enter the empty tomb.

9. He assisted in the preparation of Jesus' body for burial.

10. He doubted Jesus' resurrection.

THE MOST FAMOUS FINISH

1. Judas (John 18:2)

2. Caiaphas (Matthew 26:57)

3. Barabbas (Matthew 27:16)

4. Pilate (Matthew 27:19)

5. Joseph (Matthew 27:59, 60)

6. Elijah (Matthew 27:47)

7. Simon (Matthew 27:32)

8. Peter (John 20:6)

9. Nicodemus (John 19:39)

10. Thomas (John 20:25)

MORE ON THE MOST FAMOUS FINISH

Answer some more questions about Jesus' death and resurrection.

1. Where was Jesus praying when he was arrested?

2. How much was Judas paid for betraying Jesus?

3. How did Judas identify Jesus for the soldiers?

4. Jesus was found guilty by the Sanhedrin for what crime?

5. When Jesus died, what happened to the curtain in the temple?

6. Where was Jesus' tomb located?

7. When the women first saw Jesus after his resurrection, who did they think he was?

8. When the guards saw the angel at the empty tomb, what did they do?

9. What was the name of the place where Jesus was crucified?

10. At the moment of Jesus' death, who went into the holy city?

MORE ON THE MOST FAMOUS FINISH

1. Gethsemane (Matthew 26:36)

2. thirty silver coins (Matthew 26:15)

3. He kissed him. (Matthew 26:49)

4. blasphemy (Matthew 26:65)

5. It was torn in two from top to bottom. (Matthew 27:51)

6. in a garden (John 19:41)

7. the gardener (John 20:15)

8. They shook with fear. (Matthew 28:4)

9. Golgotha (Matthew 27:33)

10. dead people raised to life (Matthew 27:52, 53)

VI

MAY I
QUOTE YOU?

WHAT'S MY LINE?:
Old Testament

Can you identify the speaker of these famous Old Testament quotes?

1. "My punishment is more than I can bear. Today you are driving me from the land, and I will be hidden from your presence."

2. "Look! I see four men walking around in the fire, unbound and unharmed, and the fourth looks like a son of the gods."

3. "Give your servant a discerning heart to govern your people and to distinguish between right and wrong."

4. "The Israelites have rejected your covenant, broken down your altars, and put your prophets to death with the sword. I am the only one left, and now they are trying to kill me too."

5. "Speak, Lord, for your servant is listening."

6. "He was despised and rejected by men, a man of sorrows, and familiar with suffering."

7. "You intended to harm me, but God intended it for good to accomplish what is now being done, the saving of many lives."

8. "Choose for yourselves this day whom you will serve . . . but as for me and my household, we will serve the Lord."

9. "I know that my Redeemer lives. . . . And after my skin has been destroyed, yet in my flesh I will see God."

10. "Remember me for this, O my God, and do not blot out what I have so faithfully done for the house of my God."

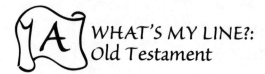

WHAT'S MY LINE?:
Old Testament

1. Cain (Genesis 4:13)

2. Nebuchadnezzar (Daniel 3:25)

3. Solomon (1 Kings 3:9)

4. Elijah (1 Kings 19:10)

5. Samuel (1 Samuel 3:9)

6. Isaiah (Isaiah 53:3)

7. Joseph (Genesis 50:20)

8. Joshua (Joshua 24:15)

9. Job (Job 19:25, 26)

10. Nehemiah (Nehemiah 13:14)

WHAT'S MY LINE?: New Testament

Can you identify the speaker of these famous New Testament quotes?

1. "What do you want with us, Jesus of Nazareth? Have you come to destroy us? I know who you are—the Holy One of God!"

2. "I don't know this man you're talking about."

3. "Sovereign Lord, as you have promised, you now dismiss your servant in peace, for my eyes have seen your salvation."

4. "Look, the Lamb of God, who takes away the sin of the world!"

5. "Unless I see the nail marks in his hands and put my finger where the nails were, and put my hand into his side, I will not believe."

6. "It is better for you that one man die for the people."

7. "For to me, to live is Christ and to die is gain."

8. "I am the Lord's servant; may it be to me as you have said."

9. "This is the disciple who testifies to these things and who wrote them down. We know that his testimony is true."

10. "Friend, do what you came for."

WHAT'S MY LINE?:
New Testament

1. a man possessed by an evil spirit (Mark 1:24)

2. Peter (Mark 14:71)

3. Simeon (Luke 2:29)

4. John the Baptist (John 1:29)

5. Thomas (John 20:25)

6. Caiaphas (John 11:50)

7. Paul (Philippians 1:21)

8. Mary (Luke 1:38)

9. John (John 21:24)

10. Jesus (Matthew 26:50)

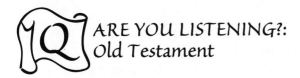

ARE YOU LISTENING?:
Old Testament

Can you identify the person to whom God spoke these Old Testament quotes? (Choices: Moses, Adam, Isaiah, Ben-Hur, Jonah, Jacob, Samuel, Abraham, Joshua, Jeremiah, Job)

1. "Cursed is the ground because of you; through painful toil you will eat of it all the days of your life."

2. "Before I formed you in the womb I knew you, before you were born I set you apart."

3. "Where were you when I laid the earth's foundation?"

4. "Be strong and courageous, because you will lead these people to inherit the land I swore to their forefathers to give them."

5. "I will bless those who bless you, and whoever curses you I will curse; and all peoples on earth will be blessed through you."

6. "I AM WHO I AM. This is what you are to say to the Israelites: 'I AM has sent me to you.'"

7. "I will give you and your descendants the land on which you are lying."

8. "Go to the great city of Nineveh and preach against it."

9. "Whom shall I send? And who will go for us?"

10. "The Lord does not look at the things man looks at. Man looks at the outward appearance, but the Lord looks at the heart."

 ARE YOU LISTENING?:
Old Testament

1. Adam (Genesis 3:17)

2. Jeremiah (Jeremiah 1:5)

3. Job (Job 38:4)

4. Joshua (Joshua 1:6)

5. Abraham (Genesis 12:3)

6. Moses (Exodus 3:14)

7. Jacob (Genesis 28:13)

8. Jonah (Jonah 1:2)

9. Isaiah (Isaiah 6:8)

10. Samuel (1 Samuel 16:7)

GREAT QUESTIONS IN THE BIBLE:
Old Testament

Who asked the following Old Testament questions?

1. "Is the man Absalom safe?"

2. "If a man dies, will he live again?"

3. "Suppose I go to the Israelites and say to them, 'The God of your fathers sent me to you,' and they ask me, 'What is his name?' Then what shall I tell them?"

4. "I don't know. Am I my brother's keeper?"

5. "The fire and the wood are here, but where is the lamb for the burnt offering?"

6. "Why didn't you tell me she was your wife? Why did you say, 'She is my sister,' so that I took her to be my wife?"

7. "Will a son be born to a man a hundred years old?"

8. "What is this you are doing for the people? Why do you alone sit as a judge, while all these people stand around you from morning to evening?"

9. "For who is able to govern this great people of yours?"

10. "O Lord my God, have you brought tragedy also upon this widow I am staying with, by causing her son to die?"

GREAT QUESTIONS IN THE BIBLE:
Old Testament

1. David (2 Samuel 18:32)

2. Job (Job 14:14)

3. Moses (Exodus 3:13)

4. Cain (Genesis 4:9)

5. Isaac (Genesis 22:7)

6. Pharaoh (Genesis 12:18, 19)

7. Abraham (Genesis 17:17)

8. Jethro (Exodus 18:14)

9. Solomon (1 Kings 3:9)

10. Elijah (1 Kings 17:20)

GREAT QUESTIONS IN THE BIBLE:
New Testament

Who asked the following New Testament questions?

1. "Sirs, what must I do to be saved?"

2. "What is truth?"

3. "What shall we say then? Shall we go on sinning that grace may increase?"

4. "Are you the one who was to come, or should we expect someone else?"

5. *"Eloi, Eloi, lama sabachthani?"*

6. "How can a man be born when he is old?"

7. "Son, why have you treated us like this? Your father and I have been anxiously searching for you."

8. "Good teacher, what must I do to inherit eternal life?"

9. "You always resist the Holy Spirit! Was there ever a prophet your fathers did not persecute?"

10. "Can anyone keep these people from being baptized with water? They have received the Holy Spirit just as we have."

GREAT QUESTIONS IN THE BIBLE:
New Testament

1.   the jailer (Acts 16:30)

2.   Pilate (John 18:38)

3.   Paul (Romans 6:1)

4.   John the Baptist (Luke 7:19)

5.   Jesus (Matthew 27:46)

6.   Nicodemus (John 3:4)

7.   Mary (Luke 2:48)

8.   the rich ruler (Luke 18:18)

9.   Stephen (Acts 7:52)

10. Peter (Acts 10:47)

 AYE, AYE, SIR!

Who received the following commands from God?

1. "March around the city once with all the armed men. Do this for six days. . . . On the seventh day, march around the city seven times."

2. "Take off your sandals."

3. "Leave here, turn eastward and hide in the Kerith Ravine, east of the Jordan."

4. "Do not consider his appearance or his height, for I have rejected him. . . . Rise and anoint him; he is the one."

5. "You are to take every kind of food that is to be eaten and store it away as food for you and for them."

6. "Take them down to the water, and I will sift them for you there."

7. "Go up to Bethel and settle there, and build an altar there to God, who appeared to you."

8. "You must not eat from the tree of the knowledge of good and evil, for when you eat of it you will surely die."

9. "Do not go down to Egypt; live in the land where I tell you to live. . . . I will be with you and will bless you."

10. "Do not lay a hand on the boy. Do not do anything to him. Now I know that you fear God."

AYE, AYE, SIR!

1. Joshua (Joshua 6:3, 4)

2. Moses (Exodus 3:5)

3. Elijah (1 Kings 17:3)

4. Samuel (1 Samuel 16:7, 12)

5. Noah (Genesis 6:21)

6. Gideon (Judges 7:4)

7. Jacob (Genesis 35:1)

8. Adam (Genesis 2:17)

9. Isaac (Genesis 26:2, 3)

10. Abraham (Genesis 22:12)

TALKIN' TO THE BIG GUY

Who prayed the following prayers?

1. "O Sovereign Lord, what can you give me since I remain childless and the one who will inherit my estate is Eliezer of Damascus?"

2. "May the Lord, the God of the spirits of all mankind, appoint a man over this community . . . so the Lord's people will not be like sheep without a shepherd."

3. "Lord, save me!"

4. "Lord Jesus, receive my spirit. Lord, do not hold this sin against them."

5. "Jesus, Son of David, have mercy on me! Rabbi, I want to see."

6. "I put my hand over my mouth. I spoke once, but I have no answer—twice, but I will say no more."

7. "I pray that out of his glorious riches he may strengthen you with power through his Spirit in your inner being."

8. "Amen. Come, Lord Jesus."

9. "O Lord . . . I had only my staff when I crossed this Jordan, but now I have become two groups. Save me, I pray, from the hand of my brother . . . for I am afraid."

10. "I praise you, Father, Lord of heaven and earth, because you have hidden these things from the wise and learned, and revealed them to the little children."

TALKIN' TO THE BIG GUY

1.   Abraham, asking for an heir (Genesis 15:2)

2.   Moses, asking for a successor (Numbers 27:16)

3.   Peter, walking on the water (Matthew 14:30)

4.   Stephen, as he was stoned to death (Acts 7:59)

5.   Bartimaeus, the blind man (Mark 10:48–51)

6.   Job, when faced with God's questions (Job 40:4, 5)

7.   Paul, in a prayer for the Ephesians (Ephesians 3:16)

8.   John, at the conclusion of Revelation (Revelation 22:20)

9.   Jacob, as he prepares to meet Esau (Genesis 32:10, 11)

10. Jesus, after denouncing unrepentant cities (Matthew 11:25)

MORE TALKIN' TO THE BIG GUY

Who prayed the following prayers?

1. "It is true, O Lord, that the Assyrian kings have laid waste these nations. . . . Now, O Lord our God, deliver us from his hand."

2. "Will you sweep away the righteous with the wicked? What if there are fifty righteous people in the city?"

3. "The engulfing waters threatened me, the deep surrounded me; seaweed was wrapped around my head. . . . But you brought my life up from the pit, O Lord my God."

4. "Lord, save us! We're going to drown!"

5. "Now, show me your glory."

6. "Do not be angry with me. Let me make just one more request. Allow me one more test with the fleece."

7. "O God, please strengthen me just once more, and let me with one blow get revenge on the Philistines for my two eyes."

8. "Who are you, Lord?"

9. "Then I acknowledged my sin to you and did not cover up my iniquity. I said, 'I will confess my transgressions to the Lord'— and you forgave the guilt of my sin."

10. "Remember me for this, O my God, and do not blot out what I have so faithfully done for the house of my God and its services."

MORE TALKIN' TO THE BIG GUY

1. Hezekiah (2 Kings 19:17–19)

2. Abram (Genesis 18:23, 24)

3. Jonah (Jonah 2:5, 6)

4. Jesus' disciples (Matthew 8:25)

5. Moses (Exodus 33:18)

6. Gideon (Judges 6:39)

7. Samson (Judges 16:28)

8. Paul (Acts 9:5)

9. David (Psalm 32:5)

10. Nehemiah (Nehemiah 13:14)

 I PROMISE

Identify the speaker of the following vows. (Choices: Saul, God, Hannah, Jephthah, Jezebel, Peter, Jacob, Absalom, David)

1. "If God will be with me and will watch over me on this journey I am taking . . . then the Lord will be my God and this stone that I have set up as a pillar will be God's house, and of all that you give me I will give you a tenth."

2. "If the Lord takes me back to Jerusalem, I will worship the Lord in Hebron."

3. "Even if all fall away, I will not. Even If I have to die with you, I will never disown you."

4. "Consult a spirit for me, and bring up for me the one I name. As surely as the Lord lives, you will not be punished for this."

5. "May God deal with me, be it ever so severely, if I taste bread or anything else before the sun sets!"

6. "I swear by myself that . . . I will surely bless you and make your descendants as numerous as the stars in the sky."

7. "O Lord Almighty, if you will only look upon your servant's misery and remember me, and not forget your servant but give her a son, then I will give him to the Lord for all the days of his life, and no razor will ever be used on his head."

8. "May the gods deal with me, be it ever so severely, if by this time tomorrow I do not make your life like that of one of them."

I PROMISE

1. Jacob (Genesis 28:20, 21)

2. Absalom (2 Samuel 15:8)

3. Peter (Mark 14:29, 31)

4. Saul (1 Samuel 28:8, 10)

5. David (2 Samuel 3:35)

6. God (Genesis 22:16, 17)

7. Hannah (1 Samuel 1:11)

8. Jezebel (1 Kings 19:2)

PEN PALS

The Bible contains many famous letters. Can you fill in the blanks with the name of the sender, recipient, or subject of these letters?

1. TO: Joab

    FROM: _____

    SUBJECT: "Put Uriah in the front line where the fighting is fiercest. Then withdraw from him so he will be struck down and die."

2. TO: _____

    FROM: Sanballat

    SUBJECT: "It is reported among the nations . . . that you and the Jews are plotting to revolt, and therefore you are building the wall. . . . Now this report will get back to the king; so come, let us confer together."

3. TO: Jehoram

    FROM: _____

    SUBJECT: "This is what the Lord, the God of your father David, says: 'You have not walked in the ways of your father Jehoshaphat or of Asa king of Judah . . . the Lord is about to strike your people.'"

4. TO: Philemon

    FROM: Paul

    SUBJECT: "I appeal to you for my son _____, who became my son while I was in chains."

PEN PALS

1. David (2 Samuel 11:14, 15)

2. Nehemiah (Nehemiah 6:5–7)

3. Elijah (2 Chronicles 21:12–15)

4. Onesimus (Philemon 10)

MORE PEN PALS

The Bible contains many famous letters. Can you fill in the blanks with the name of the sender, recipient, or subject of these letters?

1. TO: The officials of Jezreel

   FROM: _____

   SUBJECT: "If you are on my side and will obey me, take the heads of your master's sons and come to me in Jezreel by this time tomorrow."

2. TO: _____

   FROM: Claudius Lysias

   SUBJECT: "This man was seized by the Jews, . . . but I rescued him, for I had learned that he is a Roman citizen. . . . I sent him to you at once. I also ordered his accusers to present to you their case against him."

3. TO: The king of Israel

   FROM: The king of Aram

   SUBJECT: "With this letter I am sending my servant _____ to you so that you may cure him of his leprosy."

4. TO: The church in Philadelphia

   FROM: _____

   SUBJECT: "These are the words of him who is holy and true, who holds the key of David. What he opens no one can shut, and what he shuts no one can open."

MORE PEN PALS

1.   Jehu (2 Kings 10:6)

2.   Governor Felix (Acts 23:25–30)

3.   Naaman (2 Kings 5:5, 6)

4.   Jesus (Revelation 3:7)

VII

FAMILY
MATTERS

HERE COMES THE BRIDE

On the left is a list of brides, and on the right, their lucky mates.
Can you match each bride and groom?

1. ___ Eve   a. Joseph

2. ___ Rebekah   b. Christ

3. ___ Rachel   c. Xerxes

4. ___ Zipporah   d. Adam

5. ___ Ruth   e. Jacob

6. ___ Esther   f. Isaac

7. ___ Mary   g. Boaz

8. ___ The Church   h. Moses

9. ___ Sapphira   i. Nabal

10. ___ Abigail   j. Ananias

HERE COMES THE BRIDE

1. d. Adam (Genesis 3:20)

2. f. Isaac (Genesis 24:67)

3. e. Jacob (Genesis 29:18)

4. h. Moses (Exodus 2:21)

5. g. Boaz (Ruth 4:13)

6. c. Xerxes (Esther 2:16)

7. a. Joseph (Matthew 1:24)

8. b. Christ (Revelation 19:7)

9. j. Ananias (Acts 5:1)

10. i. Nabal (1 Samuel 25:3)

GOING TO THE CHAPEL

On the left is a list of couples, and on the right, the places where they were married. Match each couple with the place of their wedding.

1. ___ Adam and Eve   a. Persia

2. ___ Rebekah and Isaac   b. Heaven

3. ___ Rachel and Jacob   c. Bethlehem

4. ___ Zipporah and Moses   d. Beersheba

5. ___ Ruth and Boaz   e. Eden

6. ___ Esther and Xerxes   f. Haran

7. ___ Mary and Joseph   g. Midian

8. ___ The Church and Christ   h. Nazareth

GOING TO THE CHAPEL

1. e. Eden (Genesis 3:20)

2. d. Beersheba (Genesis 24:67)

3. f. Haran (Genesis 29:4, 28)

4. g. Midian (Exodus 2:21)

5. c. Bethlehem (Ruth 4:13)

6. a. Persia (Esther 2:16)

7. h. Nazareth (Luke 1:26)

8. b. Heaven (Revelation 19:7)

PUCKER UP!

Choose the correct answer to these questions about Bible smooches.

1. Who committed the greatest betrayal in the Bible with a kiss?
   a. Peter
   b. Charlton Heston
   c. Judas
   d. Moses

2. After she broke the jar of perfume, where did the woman who lived a sinful life kiss Jesus?
   a. on the nose
   b. on the feet
   c. in the kitchen
   d. on the head

3. How does Paul tell people to greet each other?
   a. with a Hershey's kiss
   b. with a holy kiss
   c. with an affectionate kiss
   d. with a gentle kiss

4. Who wanted his hairy son to come close and kiss him?
   a. Isaac
   b. Kong
   c. Abraham
   d. Esau

5. According to Proverbs, what is like a kiss on the lips?
   a. a smack in the face
   b. the words of a deceiver
   c. a cool breeze
   d. an honest answer

PUCKER UP!

1. c. Judas (Matthew 26:23)

2. b. on the feet (Luke 7:38)

3. b. with a holy kiss (1 Corinthians 16:20)

4. a. Isaac (Genesis 27:26)

5. d. an honest answer (Proverbs 24:26)

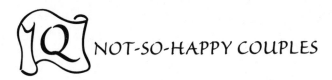 NOT-SO-HAPPY COUPLES

Answer these questions about some troubled Bible couples.

1. What tragic fate befell Lot's wife?

2. Who was beheaded for telling King Herod that he should not have his brother's wife?

3. Which king, married to Queen Bernice, asked the apostle Paul: "Do you think that in such a short time you can persuade me to be a Christian?"

4. Which prophet was not allowed to mourn at the sudden death of his wife?

5. Which prophet was commanded by God to marry the adulteress Gomer?

6. In order to cover up his adultery with Bathsheba, what did King David do to her husband?

7. Paul wrote a letter to a church, instructing them to expel a man who "has his father's wife." In what city was that church?

8. Who was King Abab's notoriously wicked queen?

9. When the Sadducees asked Jesus the question about the woman widowed seven times, what concept were they trying to disprove?

10. Which ruler, married to a Jewish woman named Drusilla, hoped the apostle Paul would offer him a bribe for his freedom?

NOT-SO-HAPPY COUPLES

1. She became a pillar of salt. (Genesis 19:26)

2. John the Baptist (Matthew 14:3–11)

3. Agrippa (Acts 26:28)

4. Ezekiel (Ezekiel 24:18)

5. Hosea (Hosea 1:2, 3)

6. He had him killed. (2 Samuel 11)

7. Corinth (1 Corinthians 5:1)

8. Jezebel (1 Kings16:30, 31)

9. the resurrection (Matthew 22:23–28)

10. Governor Felix (Acts 24:24–26)

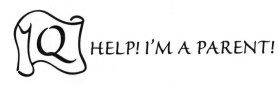

HELP! I'M A PARENT!

Test your Bible IQ with these questions about parenting in the Bible.

1. According to the Bible, having many sons is like having what?
   a. a basket full of fruit
   b. a quiver full of arrows
   c. a stable full of horses
   d. a cage full of birds

2. How does Paul instruct children to behave to their parents?
   a. respect them
   b. humor them
   c. follow them
   d. obey them

3. According to Hebrews, how does a father treat his true sons?
   a. He disciplines them.
   b. He takes them fishing.
   c. He encourages them.
   d. He respects them.

4. What promise comes with the commandment to "Honor your father and mother"?
   a. that it may go well with you
   b. that you may live long in the land
   c. that you may be delivered from the wrath of God
   d. that you may inherit your father's blessing

5. According to the apostle Paul, what must fathers avoid with their children?
   a. exasperating them
   b. listening to their music
   c. hitting them
   d. judging them

HELP! I'M A PARENT!

1. b. a quiver full of arrows (Psalm 127:3–5)

2. d. obey them (Ephesians 6:1)

3. a. He disciplines them. (Hebrews 12:7–11)

4. b. that you may live long in the land (Exodus 20:12)

5. a. exasperating them (Ephesians 6:4)

FATHERS AND SONS

On the left is a list of proud fathers, and on the right, their bouncing baby boys. Can you match the dad with his son?

1. ___ Adam   a. Jacob

2. ___ Nun   b. Solomon

3. ___ Zebedee   c. Joshua

4. ___ Jesse   d. King Saul

5. ___ King Saul   e. David

6. ___ David   f. John

7. ___ Abraham   g. Cain

8. ___ Isaac   h. Jonathan

9. ___ Zacharias   i. Isaac

10. ___ Kish   j. John the Baptist

FATHERS AND SONS

1. g. Cain (Genesis 4:1)

2. c. Joshua (Numbers 11:28)

3. f. John (Matthew 4:2)

4. e. David (1 Samuel 17:17)

5. h. Jonathan (1 Samuel 13:16)

6. b. Solomon (1 Kings 1:13)

7. i. Isaac (Genesis 21:3)

8. a. Jacob (Genesis 25:26)

9. j. John the Baptist (Luke 1:13)

10. d. King Saul (1 Samuel 9:3)

MOTHERS AND SONS

On the left is a list of sons, and on the right, their mothers. Can you match the son with his mom?

1. ___ Isaac	a. Bilhah
2. ___ Abel	b. Bathsheba
3. ___ Jacob	c. Eunice
4. ___ Reuben	d. Rebekah
5. ___ Dan	e. Elizabeth
6. ___ Joseph	f. Hannah
7. ___ John the Baptist	g. Eve
8. ___ Solomon	h. Leah
9. ___ Samuel	i. Sarah
10. ___ Timothy	j. Rachel

MOTHERS AND SONS

1. i. Sarah (Genesis 21:3)

2. g. Eve (Genesis 4:1)

3. d. Rebekah (Genesis 25:21–26)

4. h. Leah (Genesis 29:32)

5. a. Bilhah (Genesis 30:4–6)

6. j. Rachel (Genesis 30:23, 24)

7. e. Elizabeth (Luke 1:57–63)

8. b. Bathsheba (1 Kings 1:11)

9. f. Hannah (1 Samuel 1:20)

10. c. Eunice (2 Timothy 1:5)

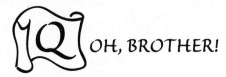

OH, BROTHER!

Can you match the Bible brothers?

1.	___ James	a.	Esau
2.	___ Andrew	b.	James
3.	___ Aaron	c.	Abishai
4.	___ Jacob	d.	Abel
5.	___ Joseph	e.	Philip
6.	___ Jesus	f.	Benjamin
7.	___ Cain	g.	John
8.	___ Nahor	h.	Moses
9.	___ Herod	i.	Abraham
10.	___ Joab	j.	Peter

OH, BROTHER!

1. g. John (Matthew 4:21)

2. j. Peter (Matthew 4:18)

3. h. Moses (Exodus 6:20)

4. a. Esau (Genesis 25:25)

5. f. Benjamin (Genesis 35:24)

6. b. James (Mark 6:3)

7. d. Abel (Genesis 4:2)

8. i. Abraham (Genesis 22:23)

9. e. Philip (Matthew 14:3)

10. c. Abishai (2 Samuel 3:30)

 KID STUFF

Answer these questions about kids in the Bible.

1. What couple's infant son died as punishment for their adultery?

2. What did King Solomon propose doing to a baby in order to settle a dispute between two prostitutes who both claimed to be the child's mother?

3. What did Jesus do to Jairus's daughter?

4. Who was Rhoda (Mary's servant girl) so excited to see at the door that she forgot to open it to let him in?

5. According to Jesus, what will children do to their parents at the end of the age?

6. What problem did a young boy have that Jesus' disciples were unable to do anything about?

7. What did Jonathan have a young boy do as a signal to David that he was safe from King Saul?

8. In addition to praying, what did Elijah do to a young boy to bring him back to life?

9. According to Jesus, if anyone causes a child who believes in Him to sin, it would be better for that person to have what happen to him?

10. What child was described as "growing in wisdom and stature, and in favor with God and men"?

 KID STUFF

1. David and Bathsheba (2 Samuel 12:15–18)

2. cut it in two (1 Kings 3:16–27)

3. He raised her from the dead. (Mark 5:35–42)

4. Peter (Acts 12:13)

5. They will rebel against them and have them killed. (Mark 13:12)

6. He was possessed by an evil spirit. (Mark 9:24)

7. look for arrows (1 Samuel 20:21)

8. He stretched himself out on the boy three times. (1 Kings 17:19–21)

9. to have a large millstone hung around his neck and be drowned in the depths of the sea (Matthew 18:5, 6)

10. Jesus (Luke 2:52)

REAL MEN DO CRY

On the left is a list of Biblical men who cried, and on the right, the occasions for their crying. Can you match the man with the reason he shed his tears?

1. ___ Abraham

2. ___ Esau

3. ___ Jacob

4. ___ Joseph

5. ___ Saul

6. ___ David

7. ___ Elisha

8. ___ Hezekiah

9. ___ Peter

10. ___ Jesus

a. the destruction of Ziklag

b. meeting Rachel

c. Sarah's death

d. the future cruelty of King Hazael

e. Lazarus's death

f. when David did not kill him

g. He was reunited with his brothers.

h. The rooster crowed and he realized he had disowned Jesus.

i. his brother's treachery

j. Isaiah told him he was going to die.

A REAL MEN DO CRY

1. c. Sarah's death (Genesis 23:2)

2. i. his brother's treachery (Genesis 27:34)

3. b. meeting Rachel (Genesis 29:11)

4. g. He was reunited with his brothers. (Genesis 45:14, 15)

5. f. when David did not kill him (1 Samuel 24:16)

6. a. the destruction of Ziklag (1 Samuel 30:4)

7. d. the future cruelty of King Hazael (2 Kings 8:11, 12)

8. j. Isaiah told him he was going to die. (2 Kings 20:1–3)

9. h. The rooster crowed and he realized he had disowned Jesus. (Luke 22:60–62)

10. e. Lazarus's death (John 11:35)

VIII

THE DAILY GRIND

 DRESS FOR SUCCESS

Test your Bible knowledge with these questions about the finest in Biblical fashions.

1. Whose father made him a "richly ornamented robe"?

2. What was John the Baptist's clothing made of?

3. What did God use to make garments for Adam and Eve?

4. Whose clothes did God instruct Moses to make using "gold, and blue, purple and scarlet yarn, and fine linen"?

5. Who brought judgment on Israel by keeping a "beautiful robe from Babylonia"?

6. What was the color of the robe the soldiers placed on Jesus as they mocked him?

7. In addition to a robe, what else did the father put on the returned prodigal son?

8. What were "the souls of those who had been slain because of the word of God" given to wear?

9. What did Jeroboam do to the prophet Ahijah's new cloak?

10. When Peter saw Jesus standing on the shore, what did he do after putting on his outer garment?

DRESS FOR SUCCESS

1. Joseph (Genesis 37:3)

2. camel's hair (Mark 1:6)

3. skins (Genesis 3:21)

4. the high priest's (Exodus 28:5)

5. Achan (Joshua 7:21)

6. scarlet (Matthew 27:28)

7. sandals and a ring (Luke 15:22)

8. white robes (Revelation 6:9–11)

9. He tore it into twelve pieces. (1 Kings 11:30)

10. He jumped into the water. (John 21:7)

 MORE DRESS FOR SUCCESS

Answer some more questions about the clothing worn in the Bible.

1. What naughty woman snatched Joseph's cloak when he fled from her house to avoid her advances?

2. Who was the young man following when he fled naked into the night, leaving his garment behind?

3. On whom did Moses put Aaron's garments just before Aaron died?

4. Who said, "Spread the corner of your garment over me, since you are a kinsman-redeemer"?

5. In Jesus' parable, what happened to the man who showed up at the wedding banquet wearing the wrong clothes?

6. What did Jonathan do with his robe to seal his friendship with David?

7. In addition to scrolls and parchments, what article of clothing did the apostle Paul leave in Troas and later ask Timothy to bring him?

8. What was it about Jesus' undergarment that led the soldiers to cast lots for it rather than tear it?

9. Instead of killing him, David cut off a corner of the robe of what man?

10. Why did David dance in a linen ephod?

MORE DRESS FOR SUCCESS

1. Potiphar's wife (Genesis 39:12)

2. Jesus (Mark 14:51, 52)

3. Aaron's son, Eleazar (Numbers 20:28)

4. Ruth (Ruth 3:9)

5. He was tied hand and foot and thrown outside into the darkness. (Matthew 22:11–13)

6. He gave it to David. (1 Samuel 18:4)

7. a cloak (2 Timothy 4:13)

8. It was seamless. (John 19:23, 24)

9. Saul (1 Samuel 24:11)

10. The ark of the covenant was being brought into Jerusalem. (1 Chronicles 15:28, 29)

 FUN WITH FOOD

Can you answer these questions about eating and drinking in the Bible?

1. What did Jacob trade for his brother's birthright?

2. What strange diet did John the Baptist eat?

3. What substance did Moses command the Israelites to drink?

4. When Jesus was talking to the Samaritan woman, what did he say was his food?

5. What inedible item tasted like honey to Ezekiel?

6. What did God give the Israelites to eat in the desert?

7. When the prodigal son returned home, what did they eat to celebrate?

8. What place was described as flowing with milk and honey?

9. What did Jesus describe himself as?

10. What did Jesus say that a loving father would never give to his son in place of a fish?

FUN WITH FOOD

1. bread and stew (Genesis 25:34)

2. locusts and wild honey (Matthew 3:4)

3. gold dust from the golden calf (Exodus 32:20)

4. to do the Father's will and finish his work (John 4:34)

5. a scroll (Ezekiel 3:1)

6. manna and quail (Exodus 16)

7. fattened calf (Luke 15:23)

8. the promised land (Exodus 3:8)

9. bread (John 6:35)

10. a snake (Luke 11:11)

DON'T EAT THAT!

Can you answer these questions about forbidden foods in the Bible?

1. The Christians in Corinth questioned the apostle Paul about eating what kind of meat?
   a. pork
   b. meat sacrificed to idols
   c. meat sacrificed in the Jewish Temple
   d. Spam

2. What part of the animal were the Israelites not allowed to eat?
   a. the heart
   b. the head
   c. the feet
   d. the blood

3. The Council at Jerusalem decided that Christians should abstain from what kind of meat?
   a. meat from starved animals
   b. meat from strangled animals
   c. meat from stabbed animals
   d. road kill

4. Which of these bugs were the Israelites allowed to eat?
   a. beetles
   b. grasshoppers
   c. praying mantis
   d. butterflies

5. What bird were the Israelites not allowed to eat?
   a. eagle
   b. turkey
   c. chicken
   d. dove

DON'T EAT THAT!

1. b. meat sacrificed to idols (1 Corinthians 10:23–30)

2. d. the blood (Leviticus 17:10)

3. b. meat from strangled animals (Acts 15:20)

4. b. grasshoppers (Leviticus 11:20)

5. a. eagle (Leviticus 11:13)

BIBLE BISTRO

Test your knowledge of famous Biblical feasts with these questions.

1. Who liked to tell riddles at his wedding feast?

2. Who was Joseph so happy to see that he gave a feast?

3. Where was the wedding feast held where Jesus turned water into wine?

4. For whom did Abraham prepare a feast near the great trees of Mamre?

5. Solomon held a great feast to celebrate what event?

6. Who refused to participate in the feast celebrating the return of the prodigal son?

7. What queen was deposed because she refused to dance before the drunken king and his guests?

8. Whose sons and daughters were killed during a feast?

9. Who held the feast where Jesus was criticized for eating with tax collectors and sinners?

10. What kind of feast will the Lamb have at the end of time?

BIBLE BISTRO

1. Samson (Judges 14:10–14)

2. his brother, Benjamin (Genesis 43:16)

3. Cana (John 2:1–12)

4. three angels (Genesis 18:1–8)

5. to dedicate the temple in Jerusalem (1 Kings 8:65)

6. the older brother (Luke 15:22)

7. Vashti (Esther 1:10–19)

8. Job's (Job 1:18, 19)

9. Levi (Luke 5:29)

10. a wedding feast (Revelation 19:7–9)

 WINE TIME

Answer these questions about one of the most common beverages in the Bible.

1. What did the Good Samaritan use wine to do?

2. What New Testament person was strictly prohibited from drinking wine?

3. Who did the apostle Paul instruct to drink a little wine for the sake of his stomach?

4. Why were the disciples suspected of having drunk too much wine on the day of Pentecost?

5. At the wedding at Cana, who told Jesus that they were out of wine?

6. What were Aaron and his sons told to drink no wine before doing?

7. When did Jesus drink sour wine?

8. To what people was Paul referring when he told Timothy that they should not be addicted to wine?

9. According to Jesus, why should new wine not be put into old wineskins?

10. To whom did Nehemiah give wine?

 WINE TIME

1. He applied it to the traveler's wounds. (Luke 10:34)

2. John the Baptist (Luke 1:15)

3. Timothy (1 Timothy 5:23)

4. They were speaking in other tongues. (Acts 2:13)

5. his mother (John 2:3)

6. entering the Tent of Meeting (Leviticus 10:8)

7. at his crucifixion (John 19:29)

8. elders and deacons (1 Timothy 3:3–8)

9. They will burst. (Matthew 9:16)

10. King Artaxerxes (Nehemiah 2:1)

TOO MUCH TO DRINK

Choose the correct answer to these questions about wine—and the Bible people who drank too much of it!

1. What did Noah do after he had had too much to drink?
   a. He lay down to sleep it off.
   b. He lay uncovered inside his tent.
   c. He lay with his son's wife.
   d. He ran the ark aground.

2. What did Lot's daughters do after they got their father drunk?
   a. They stole his gold.
   b. They ran away.
   c. They had sex with him.
   d. They killed him.

3. What happened to Elah, King of Israel, when he was drunk?
   a. He was assassinated.
   b. He fell into a deep sleep.
   c. He saw a vision.
   d. He fell out of his chair.

4. What kind of goblets were King Belshazzar and his guests drinking from when the fingers of a hand wrote on the wall?
   a. goblets from Babylon
   b. goblets from Kmart
   c. goblets from Rome
   d. goblets from the temple in Jerusalem

5. What kind of water did Jesus change into wine?
   a. water from the Jordan river
   b. wash water
   c. holy water
   d. rainwater

TOO MUCH TO DRINK

1. b. He lay uncovered inside his tent. (Genesis 9:21)

2. c. They had sex with him. (Genesis 19:30–36)

3. a. He was assassinated. (1 Kings 16:9, 10)

4. d. goblets from the temple in Jerusalem (Daniel 5:2)

5. b. wash water (John 2:6)

 FAST FACTS

Identify the person described in each of these stories about fasting.

1. He stayed on a mountain forty days and forty nights, eating no bread and drinking no water.

2. He pleaded with God to spare a child's life, fasting and spending the nights lying on the ground.

3. This evil king felt such remorse upon hearing from a prophet how he would be punished for his evil ways that he tore his clothes, put on sackcloth, and fasted.

4. He spent the night without food or entertainment because he was worried about a young man locked up with a lion.

5. She asked the Jews in Susa to join her in a three-day fast before she went illegally to the king with a request.

6. When he heard about the condition of the Jews returning from exile and about the condition of the walls of Jerusalem, he mourned and fasted and prayed before God.

7. She worshiped night and day in the temple, fasting and praying as she looked forward to the redemption of Jerusalem.

8. The Holy Spirit led him into the desert, where he fasted forty days and forty nights.

9. He fasted for three days after a light from heaven blinded him.

10. This man's disciples once questioned Jesus about his fasting practices.

FAST FACTS

1. Moses (Deuteronomy 9:9)

2. David (2 Samuel 12:16)

3. Ahab (1 Kings 21:27)

4. Darius (Daniel 6:18)

5. Esther (Esther 4:15, 16)

6. Nehemiah (Nehemiah 1:4)

7. Anna (Luke 2:37)

8. Jesus (Matthew 4:2)

9. Paul (Acts 9:9)

10. John the Baptist (Matthew 9:14)

GETTING AROUND

Answer these questions about Bible journeys and means of travel.

1. Who was sold to a group of Ishmaelites traveling by caravan to Egypt?

2. What kind of animal did Abigail ride when she went to meet David and plead for Nabal's life?

3. Which king had twelve thousand horses?

4. Which prophet was taken up in a whirlwind accompanied by a chariot of fire?

5. Who allowed Joseph to ride in his second chariot?

6. What kind of animal did Jesus ride when he entered Jerusalem?

7. What kind of animal did Moses place his wife and sons on to take them back to Egypt?

8. What kind of animal did Ben-Hadad escape on after a battle with the Israelites?

9. What seaport city was Paul's last stop before entering Jerusalem?

10. How many navies did King Solomon have?

GETTING AROUND

1. Joseph (Genesis 37:28)

2. a donkey (1 Samuel 25:20)

3. Solomon (1 Kings 10:26)

4. Elijah (2 Kings 2:11)

5. Pharaoh (Genesis 41:43)

6. a donkey (John 12:14)

7. a donkey (Exodus 4:20)

8. a horse (1 Kings 20:20)

9. Caesarea (Acts 21:8)

10. two (1 Kings 9:22)

SOMEBODY CALL A DOCTOR!

Answer these questions about Biblical maladies and the people who cured them.

1. Who does Paul call "our dear friend, the doctor"?

2. Of what disease did Jesus heal ten men, only one of whom returned to thank him?

3. Jesus healed a blind man in Bethsaida by putting what in the man's eyes?

4. What did God cause to break out on the Philistines in Ashdod after they brought the ark into the temple of their god?

5. What did Jesus put in the deaf man's ear in order to heal him?

6. Jesus got into trouble with Pharisees because he healed a man with what problem on the Sabbath?

7. Of what medical problem did Jesus heal both Peter's mother-in-law and the son of a royal official?

8. A woman was suffering from what problem for twelve years before she touched Jesus' cloak and was healed?

9. In ancient Israel, who was responsible for determining whether or not a disease was healed?

10. An invalid lay beside the pool of Bethesda for thirty-eight years waiting for what to happen?

SOMEBODY CALL A DOCTOR!

1. Luke (Colossians 4:14)

2. leprosy (Luke 17:12–19)

3. spit (Mark 8:23)

4. tumors (1 Samuel 5:6)

5. his finger (Mark 7:32–35)

6. a shriveled hand (Matthew 12:9–14)

7. a fever (Matthew 8:14, 15; John 4:52)

8. a bleeding (Matthew 9:20)

9. the priests (Leviticus 13)

10. for someone to help him into the pool when the water was stirred (John 5:1–8)

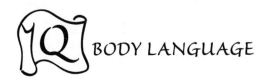 BODY LANGUAGE

Test your Bible knowledge with these questions about the body.

1. According to James, what part of the body is like a fire?

2. In Isaiah's vision, what two parts of their bodies did the seraphs cover with their wings?

3. What did the prophets of Baal on Mount Carmel do to their bodies when they got no response to their frantic prophesying?

4. In his letter to Timothy, Paul says that young men should lift up what part of their body when they pray?

5. The Lord rebukes people who only honor him with what part of their body?

6. What body part does Paul call "beautiful" on those who bring the good news?

7. According to the book of Proverbs, stirring up anger produces strife, just as the twisting of what produces blood?

8. When the men of Judah captured Adoni-Bezek, what parts of his body did they cut off?

9. Samson's strength was connected with what part of his body?

10. If the Church is a body, what part of the body is Christ?

BODY LANGUAGE

1. the tongue (James 3:6)

2. their faces and their feet (Isaiah 6:2)

3. They slashed themselves with swords and spears. (1 Kings 18:28)

4. holy hands (1 Timothy 2:8)

5. their lips (Isaiah 29:13)

6. the feet (Romans 10:15)

7. the nose (Proverbs 30:33)

8. his thumbs and big toes (Judges 1:7)

9. his hair (Judges 16:19)

10. the head (Colossians 1:18)

IX

ON THE
JOB

 NINE TO FIVE

On the left is a list of laborers, and on the right, their choice of profession. Can you match the person with his or her job?

1. ___ Paul   a. doctor

2. ___ David   b. tax collector

3. ___ Jesus   c. tentmaker

4. ___ Peter   d. dealer in cloth

5. ___ Luke   e. soldier

6. ___ Matthew   f. carpenter

7. ___ Lydia   g. tanner

8. ___ Adam   h. shepherd

9. ___ Simon (not Peter)   i. gardener

10. ___ Cornelius   j. fisherman

NINE TO FIVE

1. c. tentmaker (Acts 18:3)

2. h. shepherd (1 Samuel 16:11)

3. f. carpenter (Mark 6:3)

4. j. fisherman (Matthew 4:18)

5. a. doctor (Colossians 4:14)

6. b. tax collector (Matthew 9:9)

7. d. dealer in cloth (Acts 16:14)

8. i. gardener (Genesis 2:15)

9. g. tanner (Acts 9:43)

10. e. soldier (Acts 10:1)

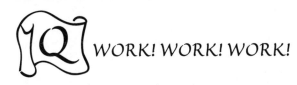 WORK! WORK! WORK!

Choose the correct answer to these questions about Biblical jobs.

1. This guy was in jail with Joseph and then was hung. He was a
   a. butcher.
   b. baker.
   c. candlestick maker.
   d. picture framer.

2. This guy did time with Joseph, too, but he managed to avoid getting hung. He was Pharaoh's
   a. chief cupbearer.
   b. chief armor-bearer.
   c. chief grizzly-bearer.
   d. chief standard-bearer.

3. The people of Israel were slaves to the Egyptians. They were forced to make
   a. baskets.
   b. brooms.
   c. bricks.
   d. boats.

4. When Demetrius wasn't causing riots in Ephesus, he was a
   a. coppersmith.
   b. blacksmith.
   c. willsmith.
   d. silversmith.

5. Zacchaeus knew how to make a buck. He was a
   a. banker.
   b. merchant.
   c. tax collector.
   d. sports agent.

WORK! WORK! WORK!

1. b. baker. (Genesis 40:22)

2. a. chief cupbearer. (Genesis 40:21)

3. c. bricks. (Exodus 1:14)

4. d. silversmith. (Acts 19:24)

5. c. tax collector. (Luke 19:2)

MORE WORK! WORK! WORK!

Labor over some more questions about Biblical vocations.

1. In Samaria, Simon practiced his trade in
    a. sorcery.
    b. law.
    c. medicine.
    d. the clarinet.

2. The apostle Paul warns Timothy to be on guard against Alexander the
    a. Great.
    b. metalworker.
    c. temple worker.
    d. high priest.

3. Mary's husband Joseph worked as a
    a. shepherd.
    b. innkeeper.
    c. carpenter.
    d. fisherman.

4. Before Onesimus relocated, he was a
    a. seaman.
    b. slave.
    c. traveling salesman.
    d. herder.

5. This man worked for Candace, queen of the Ethiopians. He was in charge of her
    a. stables.
    b. army.
    c. flocks.
    d. treasury.

MORE WORK! WORK! WORK!

1. a. sorcery. (Acts 8:9)

2. b. metalworker. (2 Timothy 4:14)

3. c. carpenter. (Matthew 13:55)

4. b. slave. (Philemon 16)

5. d. treasury. (Acts 8:27)

 POOR FOLKS

Can you answer these questions about people who didn't (or couldn't) work—the poor?

1. According to Jesus, what belongs to the poor in spirit?

2. To help a poor widow to pay her debts, what did Elisha miraculously increase?

3. Jesus commended a poor woman for putting how much money in the treasury?

4. According to Jesus, how long will poor people be around?

5. What did Peter do for the beggar, rather than give him silver and gold?

6. Who was the woman, restored to life by Peter, who was known for helping the poor?

7. According to the apostle Paul, what is it better to have than to give all our possessions to the poor?

8. From the scroll of what prophet did Jesus read: "The Spirit of the Lord is on me, because he has anointed me to preach good news to the poor"?

9. James describes his readers as poor in the eyes of the world, but rich in what?

10. What were the Israelites prohibited from taking from their poor countrymen?

POOR FOLKS

1. the kingdom of heaven (Matthew 5:3)

2. oil (2 Kings 4:1–7)

3. two small copper coins (Mark 12:42)

4. always (Mark 14:7)

5. He healed him. (Acts 3:1–8)

6. Dorcas (Acts 9:36)

7. love (1 Corinthians 13:3)

8. Isaiah (Luke 4:16–19)

9. faith (James 2:5)

10. interest (Leviticus 25:36)

 FIGHTING MEN

Can you answer these questions about soldiers, armies, and other military matters?

1. Who told a group of soldiers: "Don't extort money and don't accuse people falsely—be content with your pay"?

2. Who led David's armies?

3. Who did the apostle Paul tell to be "a good soldier of Christ Jesus"?

4. Which of the twelve tribes of Israel was exempt from military service?

5. What was the rank of the soldier who said to Jesus: "For I myself am a man under authority . . . "?

6. Who chose soldiers for a mission by seeing which men knelt to drink water and which lapped with their tongues like a dog?

7. Who sang the song that includes this line: "The Lord is a warrior; the Lord is his name. Pharaoh's chariots and his army he has hurled into the sea."?

8. Which king of Israel did God consider too warlike to build a temple for the Lord?

9. Who was guarded by two soldiers while in prison before being rescued by an angel?

10. At whose grave did soldiers shake with fear?

FIGHTING MEN

1. John the Baptist (Luke 3:14)

2. Joab (2 Samuel 20:23)

3. Timothy (2 Timothy 2:3)

4. Levi (Numbers 1:45–50)

5. Centurion (Matthew 8:9)

6. Gideon (Judges 7:5, 6)

7. Moses (Exodus 15:3, 4)

8. David (1 Chronicles 22:8)

9. Peter (Acts 12:6)

10. Jesus (Matthew 28:4)

 MORE ON FIGHTING MEN

Identify the person associated with each of the following statements about soldiers, warriors, and other aggressive sorts. (Choices: Zoro, Simeon, Jonathan, Herod, Balaam, Joshua, Saul, Goliath, Jesus, Peter, David)

1. "His spear shaft was like a weaver's rod, and its iron point weighed six hundred shekels."

2. He hacked off the ear of the high priest's servant, Malchus.

3. He and his donkey met an angel with a drawn sword.

4. He held out his javelin until all who lived in Ai were destroyed.

5. This man and his brother Levi avenged their sister's defilement by killing with the sword every Shechemite male.

6. He took a spear and a water jug from Saul as he slept.

7. This poor prince's own father threw a spear at him, trying to kill him.

8. The Philistines were going to capture him, so he ran himself through with his own sword.

9. He had James, the brother of John, put to death with the sword.

10. "Out of his mouth comes a sharp sword with which to strike down the nations."

MORE ON FIGHTING MEN

1. Goliath (1 Samuel 17:7)

2. Peter (John 18:10)

3. Balaam (Numbers 22:23)

4. Joshua (Joshua 8:26)

5. Simeon (Genesis 34:25–29)

6. David (1 Samuel 26:12)

7. Jonathan (1 Samuel 20:33)

8. Saul (1 Samuel 31:4)

9. Herod (Acts 12:1, 2)

10. Jesus (Revelation 19:15)

 WRITER'S BLOCK

Answer these questions about the people who kept themselves busy writing different Bible books.

1. Who wrote the majority of the Psalms?

2. Who wrote the Book of Proverbs?

3. What prophet wrote the Book of Isaiah?

4. Who wrote 1 and 2 Timothy?

5. Who wrote the last book of the Bible, Revelation?

6. Who wrote the Acts of the Apostles?

7. To whom is the Song of Songs attributed?

8. Who wrote Philippians?

9. Under whose inspiration were the Scriptures written?

10. Who wrote the letter to the Hebrews?

WRITER'S BLOCK

1. David

2. Solomon (Proverbs 1:1)

3. Isaiah (Isaiah 1:1)

4. Paul (1 Timothy 1:1)

5. John (Revelation 1:1)

6. Luke (Luke 1:1–4; Acts 1:1, 2)

7. Solomon (Song of Songs 1:1)

8. Paul (Philippians 1:1)

9. God's (2 Timothy 3:16)

10. The author is unknown.

SHOW ME THE MONEY

*Once workers in the Bible got paid, they had to figure out what to do
with their earnings. Test your Bible IQ with these questions about
money matters.*

1. According to the apostle Paul, what is the problem with
    loving money?

2. What financial vice is equated with idolatry?

3. What kind of giver does God love?

4. What does Jesus specifically say about God and money?

5. In the parable of the talents, what did the servant do with his
    single talent that earned him condemnation from his master?

6. How much interest were the Israelites allowed to charge their
    countrymen?

7. When Jesus sent out the twelve disciples on a preaching
    mission, how much spending money did he tell them to take?

8. What did Simon the sorcerer do that produced this response
    from Peter: "May your money perish with you"?

9. What debt did the apostle Paul tell the Christians in Rome
    that they must continually leave outstanding?

10. What is the deposit that guarantees the Christian's inheritance
    in the life to come?

SHOW ME THE MONEY

1. "The love of money is a root of all kinds of evil." (1 Timothy 6:10)

2. greed (Colossians 3:5)

3. a cheerful giver (2 Corinthians 9:7)

4. "You cannot serve both God and Money." (Matthew 6:24)

5. He hid it. (Matthew 25:25–30)

6. none (Deuteronomy 23:19)

7. none (Mark 6:8)

8. He offered Peter money in exchange for the power to bestow the Holy Spirit on people. (Acts 8:18–24)

9. the debt to love one another (Romans 13:8)

10. the Holy Spirit (Ephesians 1:13, 14)

X

POLITICS
AS USUAL

HERE COMES THE JUDGE

Before Israel had kings, they had judges. Identify the judge associated with each of the following legacies.

1. He had forty sons and thirty grandsons who rode on seventy donkeys. He led Israel for eight years.

2. This warrior defeated 135,000 Midianites with only three hundred men.

3. Born in Bethlehem, this judge led Israel for seven years and had thirty sons and thirty daughters who all married outside their clan.

4. He killed six hundred Philistines with an oxgoad.

5. He was the son of Puah, who was the son of Dodo, and he judged Israel for twenty-three years.

6. Since he was left-handed, he was able to kill the unsuspecting Eglon with a double-edged sword strapped to his right thigh.

7. He killed a thousand Philistines with the jawbone of a donkey and later killed more when he knocked down their temple.

8. This judge sacrificed his daughter as a burnt offering in order to satisfy a vow.

9. Before his judgeship, this judge received his cousin as a wife because he captured the city of Debir.

10. Her general, Barak, defeated the army of Sisera.

HERE COMES THE JUDGE

1.   Abdon (Judges 12:13, 14)

2.   Gideon (Judges 6–8)

3.   Ibzan (Judges 12:8–10)

4.   Shamgar (Judges 3:31)

5.   Tola (Judges 10:1)

6.   Ehud (Judges 3:20–22)

7.   Samson (Judges 13–16)

8.   Jephthah (Judges 11)

9.   Othniel (Judges 1:11–13)

10. Deborah (Judges 4–5)

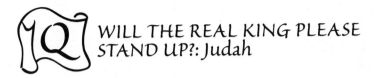

WILL THE REAL KING PLEASE STAND UP?: Judah

In each of these questions, only one of the four names listed is really a king of Judah (Southern Kingdom). Identify the true king.

1. Jeremiah, Isaiah, Rehoboam, Utellum

2. Job, Asa, Uzi, Masa

3. Jehoshaphat, Ezra, Whathephat, Maacah

4. Decorum, Memucan, Aaron, Jehoram

5. Amaziah, Graciah, Absalom, Jacob

6. Buzziah, Cuzziah, Uzziah, Nuzziah

7. Jotham, Gothum, Siddim, Shalman

8. Abram, Ahaz, Amam, Amen

9. Elmira, Zachariah, Hezekiah, Obadiah

10. Manayunk, Mareshah, Messiah, Manasseh

WILL THE REAL KING PLEASE STAND UP?: Judah

1. Rehoboam (1 Kings 12)

2. Asa (1 Kings 15:8–14)

3. Jehoshaphat (1 Kings 22:41–50)

4. Jehoram (2 Kings 8:16–24)

5. Amaziah (2 Kings 14:1–20)

6. Uzziah (2 Chronicles 26:1)

7. Jotham (2 Kings 15:32–38)

8. Ahaz (2 Kings 16:1–20)

9. Hezekiah (2 Kings 18–20)

10. Manasseh (2 Kings 21:1–18)

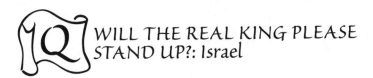

WILL THE REAL KING PLEASE STAND UP?: Israel

In each of these questions, only one of the four names listed is really a king of Israel (Northern Kingdom). Identify the true king.

1. Jehubbah, Jeroboam, Johanan, Jezaniah

2. Bildad, Nadab, Abihu, Yahoo

3. Baasha, Smaasha, Raasha, Craasha

4. Zena, Zimri, Ziphah, Zoheth

5. Rahab, Rehab, Ahab, Amad

6. Lulu, Jehu, Rehu, Mehu

7. Raamah, Jehoahaz, Jabneel, Rehoboth

8. Shallum, Willum, Canum, Shouldum

9. Boyahem, Menahem, Guyahem, Ladahem

10. Jekahiah, Nekehiah, Pekahiah, Rekahiah

WILL THE REAL KING PLEASE STAND UP?: Israel

1. Jeroboam (1 Kings 11:26)

2. Nadab (1 Kings 15:25–28)

3. Baasha (1 Kings 15:27)

4. Zimri (1 Kings 16:9–20)

5. Ahab (1 Kings 16:28–22:40)

6. Jehu (2 Kings 9:1–10)

7. Jehoahaz (2 Kings 13:1–9)

8. Shallum (2 Kings 15:10–15)

9. Menahem (2 Kings 15:14–22)

10. Pekahiah (2 Kings 15:22–26)

THOSE OTHER KINGS

On the left is a list of foreign kings (not from Israel), and on the right, their claims to fame. Can you match the king with the thing he was famous for?

1. ___ Agag

2. ___ Sennacherib

3. ___ Belshazzar

4. ___ Neco

5. ___ Herod

6. ___ Cyrus

7. ___ Nebuchadnezzar

8. ___ Abimelech

9. ___ Darius

10. ___ Augustus

a. Abraham lied to him about Sarah.

b. He issued a return decree for the Jews.

c. He was spared by Saul, but killed by Samuel.

d. He was emperor at the time of Jesus' birth.

e. He destroyed Jerusalem.

f. He ordered Daniel thrown to the lions.

g. He killed King Josiah.

h. He saw the handwriting on the wall.

i. His armies were destroyed by the Lord's angel.

j. He killed John the Baptist.

THOSE OTHER KINGS

1. c. He was spared by Saul, but killed by Samuel. (1 Samuel 15)

2. i. His armies were destroyed by the Lord's angel. (2 Kings 18–19)

3. h. He saw the handwriting on the wall. (Daniel 5)

4. g. He killed King Josiah. (2 Kings 23:29, 30)

5. j. He killed John the Baptist. (Matthew 14:1–11)

6. b. He issued a return decree for the Jews. (Ezra 1)

7. e. He destroyed Jerusalem. (2 Kings 25)

8. a. Abraham lied to him about Sarah. (Genesis 20)

9. f. He ordered Daniel thrown to the lions. (Daniel 6)

10. d. He was emperor at the time of Jesus' birth. (Luke 2)

 QUEEN FOR A DAY

Identify the queen described in each of the following statements.
(Choices: Jezebel, Candace, Michal, the Queen of Sheba, Esther,
Vashti, Elizabeth, Athaliah, Herodias, Bathsheba, Maacah)

1. She was a disobedient Persian queen deposed by King Xerxes.

2. This Ethiopian queen allowed her servant, a eunuch, to visit Judea, where he met Philip.

3. Wife of Herod Antipas, this queen plotted the death of John the Baptist.

4. She was a Jewish maiden who became the wife of King Xerxes.

5. She was the daughter of Saul who became David's first wife.

6. Originally the wife of Uriah, this queen became David's wife and was the mother of Solomon.

7. King Asa deposed this woman (who was his grandmother) from her position as queen mother because she made an Asherah pole.

8. King Ahab married this notoriously wicked and idolatrous woman.

9. This queen had most of the royal family murdered. She was eventually executed as she left the temple.

10. This visiting queen was overwhelmed with Solomon's wisdom and the splendor of his royal court.

QUEEN FOR A DAY

1. Vashti (Esther 1)

2. Candace (Acts 8:26–29)

3. Herodias (Matthew 14:1–12)

4. Esther (Esther 2–10)

5. Michal (1 Samuel 18:20–28)

6. Bathsheba (2 Samuel 11–12)

7. Maacah (2 Chronicles 15:16)

8. Jezebel (1 Kings 16:31)

9. Athaliah (2 Kings 11)

10. the Queen of Sheba (1 Kings 10)

LAYING DOWN THE LAW

True or false? Decide which of the following are actually laws of ancient Israel and which are not.

1. A man must not wear women's clothing, nor a woman wear man's clothing.

2. Every seventh olive tree must remain unharvested.

3. Do not wear clothing woven from of two kinds of material.

4. Do not plow with an ox and a donkey yoked together.

5. If a man eats anything found dead or torn by wild animals, his teeth must be pulled out and thrown outside the camp.

6. Strangers and aliens may live among the people of Israel until the year of Jubilee, then they must return to their native lands.

7. If a man is found dead in a field, the elders of the closest town must wash their hands over a heifer with a broken neck.

8. If a man is attracted to a woman taken captive in war, she must burn her foreign idols and have a gold ring placed in her ear before she can become his wife.

9. The fruit of a newly planted tree must not be eaten until the fifth year.

10. If a man will not marry his dead brother's widow, she must go up to him in the presence of the elders, take off one of his sandals, and spit in his face.

LAYING DOWN THE LAW

1. True (Deuteronomy 22:5)

2. False

3. True (Leviticus 19:19)

4. True (Deuteronomy 22:10)

5. False

6. False

7. True (Deuteronomy 21:1–7)

8. False

9. True (Leviticus 19:23–25)

10. True (Deuteronomy 25:7–10)

MORE LAYING DOWN THE LAW

True or false? Decide which of the following are actually laws of ancient Israel and which are not.

1. If you come across a bird's nest beside the road, you may take the young, but be sure to let the mother go.

2. If a man has a stubborn and rebellious son who does not obey his parents, all the men of his town shall stone him to death.

3. When building a wall for your vineyard, its height must be no more than two cubits and a handbreadth.

4. Do not charge your brother interest. You may charge a foreigner interest, but not a brother Israelite.

5. When you build a new house, make a parapet around your roof so that you will not be guilty if someone falls from it.

6. If a man has two wives, the rights of the firstborn must be bestowed upon the son of the wife he loves more.

7. Do not plant two kinds of seed in your vineyard.

8. Do not cut the hair at the sides of your head or clip off the edges of your beard.

9. You must not make slaves of the people from the nations around you. Remember that you were slaves in Egypt.

10. If a man has recently married, he must not be sent to war or have any other duty laid on him for one year.

MORE LAYING DOWN THE LAW

1. True (Deuteronomy 22:6, 7)

2. True (Deuteronomy 21:18–21)

3. False

4. True (Deuteronomy 23:19)

5. True (Deuteronomy 22:8)

6. False

7. True (Deuteronomy 22:9)

8. True (Leviticus 19:27)

9. False

10. True (Deuteronomy 24:5)

XI

NATURAL WONDERS

NATURAL DISASTERS

Test your Bible IQ with these questions about various acts of nature.

1. Who was freed from prison when an earthquake shook the doors open?

2. Which type of natural disaster occurs only once in the Bible?

3. What was Jesus doing in the boat when a furious storm began?

4. A famine forced Abram to travel to what land?

5. Who asked to be thrown overboard during a bad storm?

6. In what form did God pass by Elijah?

7. What two events in Jesus' life were accompanied by earthquakes?

8. What caused the death of Job's children?

9. Which two prophets mention the earthquake during the reign of Uzziah, king of Judah?

10. Who warned King Abab of a severe famine coming to Samaria?

NATURAL DISASTERS

1. Paul (Acts 16:26)

2. flood (Genesis 6–8)

3. sleeping (Matthew 8:24)

4. Egypt (Genesis 12:10)

5. Jonah (Jonah 1:12)

6. a gentle whisper (1 Kings 19:11–13)

7. his crucifixion (Matthew 27:51) and resurrection (Matthew 28:2)

8. a wind storm (Job 1:19)

9. Amos and Zechariah (Amos 1:1 and Zechariah 14:5)

10. Elijah (1 Kings 17:1)

GOOD WOOD

In the following statements, fill in the blanks with the correct type of tree or wood.

1. The interior of Solomon's temple was lined with _____.

2. When it returned to Noah on the ark, the dove carried a leaf from a(n) _____ tree.

3. Jesus cursed a(n) _____ tree because it had no fruit.

4. When Moses entered the Tent of Testimony, he saw that Aaron's staff had sprouted the buds, blossoms, and fruit of a(n) _____ tree.

5. Absalom got his head caught in the branches of a(n) _____ tree.

6. The crowd greeted Jesus with _____ branches when he entered Jerusalem on a donkey.

7. Zacchaeus climbed a(n) _____ tree in order to get a good view of Jesus entering Jericho.

8. After making a treaty in Beersheba, Abraham planted a(n) _____ tree there and called upon the name of the Lord, the Eternal God.

9. The "Beloved" in Song of Songs writes: "Like an _____ tree among the trees of the forest is my lover among the young men."

10. The floor of Solomon's temple was covered with _____.

GOOD WOOD

1. cedar (1 Kings 6:15)

2. olive (Genesis 8:11)

3. fig (Matthew 21:18, 19)

4. almond (Numbers 17:8)

5. oak (2 Samuel 18:9)

6. palm (John 12:13)

7. sycamore (Luke 19:4)

8. tamarisk (Genesis 21:33)

9. apple (Song of Songs 2:3)

10. pine (1 Kings 6:15)

NOT JUST WALKING ON WATER

Can you answer these questions about water in the Bible?

1. What kind of event was Jesus attending when he changed water into wine?

2. How long was the earth flooded during Noah's time?

3. After Jesus calmed the storm, what did he accuse his disciples of lacking?

4. The apostle Paul and 275 other people were shipwrecked and swam to the shore of what island?

5. In the beginning, how was the earth watered before God sent rain?

6. Jesus said that no one could enter the kingdom of God without being born of water and what?

7. According the Psalmist, what man is like a tree planted by streams of water?

8. What kind of water did Jesus offer the Samaritan woman?

9. When Moses parted the waters of the Red Sea, who moved from the front of the Israelite army to the rear?

10. When Peter was walking to Jesus on the water, what scared him and caused him to sink?

NOT JUST WALKING ON WATER

1. a wedding (John 2:1–10)

2. for 150 days (Genesis 7:24)

3. faith (Luke 8:25)

4. Malta (Acts 28:1)

5. Water came up from the ground. (Genesis 2:6)

6. the Spirit (John 3:5)

7. the man who meditates on God's law (Psalm 1:2, 3)

8. living water (John 4:10)

9. the angel of God (Exodus 14:19)

10. The wind made waves. (Matthew 14:30)

ANIMAL HOUSE

In these quotes from the Old Testament, fill in the blanks with the missing animal names.

1. "The cow will feed with the bear, their young will lie down together, and the _____ will eat straw like the ox."

2. "Then the Lord opened the _____'s mouth, and she said, 'What have I done to you to make you beat me these three times?'"

3. "And the Lord commanded the _____, and it vomited Jonah onto dry land."

4. "'You will not surely die,' the _____ said to the woman."

5. "When the _____ returned to him in the evening, there in its beak was a freshly plucked olive leaf!"

6. "The _____ brought him bread and meat in the morning and bread and meat in the evening, and he drank from the brook."

7. "Can the Ethiopian change his skin or the _____ its spots?"

8. "They will soar on wings like _____; they will run and not grow weary, they will walk and not be faint."

9. "When the powerful _____ went out, they were straining to go throughout the earth. And he said, 'Go throughout the earth!' So they went throughout the earth."

ANIMAL HOUSE

1. lion (Isaiah 11:7)

2. donkey (Numbers 22:28)

3. fish (Jonah 2:10)

4. serpent (Genesis 3:4)

5. dove (Genesis 8:11)

6. ravens (1 Kings 17:6)

7. leopard (Jeremiah 13:23)

8. eagles (Isaiah 40:31)

9. horses (Zechariah 6:7)

FISH STORIES

Can you answer the following questions about fish, fishing, and fishermen?

1. Before Jesus fed five thousand people, he had five loaves and how many fish?

2. What did Jesus tell Peter that he would find in the mouth of a fish?

3. What four apostles were fishermen?

4. The people of Israel were permitted to eat only fish with what physical characteristics?

5. People were first allowed to eat fish after what Old Testament event?

6. Who cooked a breakfast of fish and bread on the shore of the Sea of Tiberias?

7. What city had a Fish Gate?

8. What king was famous for his knowledge of animals, birds, reptiles, and fish?

9. Jesus told Peter and Andrew that they would fish for what if they followed him?

10. How many large fish did Peter catch when he followed Jesus' fishing tip?

FISH STORIES

1. two (Mark 6:41)

2. a four-drachma coin (Matthew 17:27)

3. Peter, Andrew, John, James (Mark 1:16–20)

4. fins and scales (Leviticus 11:12)

5. the flood (Genesis 9:2, 3)

6. Jesus (John 21:9–14)

7. Jerusalem (Nehemiah 3:3)

8. Solomon (1 Kings 4:33)

9. men (Matthew 4:19)

10. 153 (John 21:11)

ROCK AND ROLLING STONES

Can you answer these questions about rocks and stones in the Bible?

1. What did Moses do to the rock at Meribah that resulted in water for the Israelites to drink?

2. How did God write the commandments on the two stone tablets of the Testimony?

3. After Jacob had the dream of a stairway to heaven, what did he do with the stone he used as a pillow?

4. Where did the Israelites get the twelve stones to erect the memorial on the bank of the Jordan river?

5. What did Samuel name the stone he set up between Mizpah and Shen to commemorate the Lord's help against the Philistines?

6. What very large fellow died from a blow to the head from a rock?

7. How many stones did Elijah use to build an altar to the Lord on Mount Carmel?

8. During the Feast of Dedication in Jerusalem, why did the Jews want to stone Jesus?

9. To whom did Jesus say, "On this rock, I will build my church"?

10. Who is called the chief cornerstone?

ROCK AND ROLLING STONES

1. struck it with his staff (Exodus 17:5–7)

2. with his finger (Exodus 31:18)

3. anointed it with oil (Genesis 28:18)

4. the Jordan river (Joshua 4:8, 9)

5. Ebenezer (1 Samuel 7:12)

6. Goliath (1 Samuel 17:50)

7. twelve (1 Kings 18:31)

8. He made himself out to be God. (John 10:33)

9. Peter (Matthew 16:18)

10. Jesus (Ephesians 2:20)

 GOLD STANDARD

Test your Bible knowledge with these questions concerning the most precious metal.

1. What part of the statue in Nebuchadnezzar's dream was made of gold?

2. What happened to Shadrach, Meshach, and Abednego because they would not worship the golden image made by Nebuchadnezzar?

3. Where did Aaron get the gold to make the golden calves?

4. In addition to gold tumors, what other gold objects did the Philistines send with the ark of God on its return to Israel?

5. What king of Israel also permitted Israel to worship golden calves?

6. Who gave Jesus a gift of gold?

7. In the Book of Revelation, who were seated around the throne and wearing gold crowns?

8. Who was confronted by "a man dressed in linen, with a belt of the finest gold around his waist. His body was like chrysolite, and his face like lightning"?

9. The ark of God was overlaid with what precious metal?

10. What part of the New Jerusalem will be made of gold?

GOLD STANDARD

1.   the head (Daniel 2:32)

2.   They were thrown into a furnace. (Daniel 3)

3.   earrings (Exodus 32:2)

4.   rats (1 Samuel 6:4)

5.   Jeroboam (2 Kings 10:29)

6.   the Magi (Matthew 2:11)

7.   24 elders (Revelation 4:4)

8.   Daniel (Daniel 10:4–6)

9.   gold (Exodus 25) Good guess!

10.   the street (Revelation 21:21)

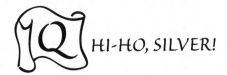

HI-HO, SILVER!

Decide whether the following statements about silver in the Bible are true or false. For extra credit, can you correct the false statements?

1. Abraham purchased the cave of Machpelah from Ephron for four hundred shekels of silver.

2. Jacob was sold to the Ishmaelites for twenty shekels of silver and taken to Egypt.

3. Joshua had two silver trumpets made to be used to call the community together and for setting out the camps.

4. Each of the Philistine rulers offered Delilah eleven hundred shekels of silver if she would betray Samson.

5. David purchased Araunah's threshing floor and oxen for fifty shekels of silver in order to sacrifice offerings there.

6. Abihu sinned against the Lord by keeping for himself plunder, which included two hundred shekels of silver.

7. Haman offered ten thousand talents of silver as a reward to men if they would drive the Jews out of Susa.

8. Hosea bought his adulterous wife out of slavery for fifteen shekels of silver.

9. The feet of the statue in Nebuchadnezzar's dream were made of silver.

10. Judas betrayed Jesus for thirty pieces of silver.

HI-HO, SILVER!

1. True (Genesis 23:14, 15)

2. False—Joseph was sold for twenty shekels. (Genesis 37:28)

3. False—Moses had the silver trumpets made. (Numbers 10:1, 2)

4. True (Judges 16:5)

5. True (2 Samuel 24:24)

6. False—Achan committed this sin. (Joshua 7:20–22)

7. False—Haman wanted the Jews destroyed. (Esther 3:9)

8. True (Hosea 3:2)

9. False—The feet were clay; the chest and arms were silver. (Daniel 2:31–33)

10. True (Matthew 26:15)

XII

SUPERNATURAL WONDERS

MIRACLE MUDDLE

Fill in the blanks in these quotes about miracles performed by Jesus.

1. "The master of the banquet tasted the _____ that had been turned into _____."

2. "A man with _____ came and knelt before him and said, 'Lord, if you are willing, you can make me clean.'"

3. "When Jesus saw their faith, he said to the _____, 'Take heart, son; your sins have been forgiven.'"

4. "He went into their synagogue and a man with a _____ _____ was there. They asked him, 'Is it lawful to heal on the Sabbath?'"

5. "Jesus replied, 'You of little faith; why are you afraid?' Then he got up and rebuked the _____ and the _____."

6. "A woman who had been subject to _____ for 12 years came up behind him and touched the edge of his cloak."

7. "But Jesus answered, 'No more of this!' And he touched the man's _____ and healed him."

8. "The demons begged Jesus, 'If you drive us out, send us into the _____ of _____.'"

9. "When they had done so, they caught such a large number of _____ that their nets began to break."

10. "Then he touched their _____ and said, 'According to your faith will it be done to you.'"

MIRACLE MUDDLE

1. water, wine (John 2:9)

2. leprosy (Matthew 8:2)

3. paralytic (Matthew 9:2)

4. shriveled hand (Matthew 12:9, 10)

5. wind, waves (Matthew 8:26)

6. bleeding (Matthew 9:20)

7. ear (Luke 22:51)

8. herd of pigs (Matthew 8:31)

9. fish (Luke 5:5, 6)

10. eyes (Matthew 9:29)

MORE MIRACLES

In each of these miraculous statements, fill in the blanks with the missing words.

1. After Pentecost, everyone in the Jerusalem church was filled with wonder because of the miracles done by the _____.

2. Elisha helped a prophet by making a borrowed _____ float.

3. God gave the _____ of Balaam the ability to speak.

4. God spoke to Moses from a burning _____.

5. The idol _____ miraculously fell on its face in the presence of the ark of God.

6. God afflicted the people of Ashdod with _____ because they had possession of the ark of God.

7. Elijah was fed by _____ while he hid in the Kerith Ravine.

8. God miraculously caused the _____ to stand still and the _____ to stop to allow the Israelites to finish their defeat of the Amorites.

9. At Marah, Moses threw a piece of _____ into the bitter water to turn the water sweet.

10. An Israelite came back to life when he was touched by Elisha's _____.

MORE MIRACLES

1. apostles (Acts 2:43)

2. axhead (2 Kings 6:6)

3. donkey (Numbers 22:28)

4. bush (Exodus 3:2)

5. Dagon (1 Samuel 5:3)

6. tumors (1 Samuel 5:6)

7. ravens (1 Kings 17:6)

8. sun, moon (Joshua 10:13)

9. wood (Exodus 15:25)

10. bones (2 Kings 13:21)

BAD NEWS FOR PHARAOH

To convince Pharaoh to let the Israelites leave Egypt, God performed many miracles. Choose the correct answer to these questions.

1. Aaron threw his staff on the ground and it became
    a. a river.
    b. a snake.
    c. an olive tree.
    d. a frog.

2. Moses struck the Nile with his staff and the water turned into
    a. ice.
    b. salt.
    c. blood.
    d. frogs.

3. Aaron struck dust with his staff and the dust became
    a. frogs.
    b. mud.
    c. dung.
    d. gnats.

4. Moses stretched out his staff toward the sky and God sent
    a. hail from the sky.
    b. snow from the sky.
    c. frogs from the sky.
    d. rain from the sky.

5. The final plague upon Egypt was the death
    a. of those stupid frogs.
    b. of all their children.
    c. of their firstborn.
    d. of Pharaoh.

BAD NEWS FOR PHARAOH

1. b. a snake. (Exodus 7:9)

2. c. blood. (Exodus 7:20)

3. d. gnats. (Exodus 8:17)

4. a. hail from the sky. (Exodus 9:23)

5. c. of their firstborn. (Exodus 12:29)

SLEEPERS AND DREAMERS

Identify the Bible character described in each of the following statements about dreams, visions, and other strange phenomena.

1. He went to sleep single, but when he awoke, he had a wife!

2. He saw a large sheet come down from heaven containing all kinds of four-footed animals, reptiles, and birds.

3. When he saw a vision of God seated on the throne surrounded by seraphs, he cried out, "Woe to me! I am ruined!"

4. He received this message in a vision: "Go to the house of Judas on Straight Street and ask for a man from Tarsus named Saul."

5. He found himself in a valley filled with dried bones that came back together when he prophesied to them.

6. An angel appeared to him in a dream and assured him that his wife had not been unfaithful to him.

7. During the night, this person had a vision of a Macedonian begging him: "Come over to Macedonia and help us."

8. He heard a voice telling him to write on a scroll what he would see and send it to seven churches.

9. God appeared to him in a dream and said, "Ask for whatever you want me to give you." God was pleased with his request.

10. God spoke to this man in a vision and told him not to be afraid to go down to Egypt.

SLEEPERS AND DREAMERS

1. Adam (Genesis 2:21–24)

2. Peter (Acts 10:9–13)

3. Isaiah (Isaiah 6:1–5)

4. Ananias (Acts 9:11)

5. Ezekiel (Ezekiel 37)

6. Joseph (Matthew 1:20, 21)

7. Paul (Acts 16:9)

8. John (Revelation 1:10, 11)

9. Solomon (1 Kings 3:5)

10. Jacob (Genesis 46:2–4)

 SHOW ME A SIGN

God would occasionally give a sign as proof or guarantee that he would fulfill his promises. Choose the correct answer to these questions about God's signs.

1. To Hezekiah, a shadow going back ten steps was a sign of what?

2. When a woman offered Abraham's servant a drink for himself and water for his camels, what was this a sign of?

3. To King Jeroboam, the splitting apart of the altar was a sign of what?

4. Who saw bread and meat consumed by fire as a sign that God was in fact speaking to him?

5. What was the sign to Moses that God really had sent him?

6. What was the sign that Abraham would be the father of many nations?

7. What sign would confirm God's judgment on Eli?

8. What would be a sign to the shepherds that a savior was born?

SHOW ME A SIGN

1. He would be healed. (2 Kings 20:9)

2. She would be Isaac's future wife. (Genesis 24:14)

3. Priests would be sacrificed on the altar. (1 Kings 13:1–3)

4. Gideon (Judges 6:17)

5. The people would worship on the mountain. (Exodus 3:12)

6. circumcision (Genesis 17:1–11)

7. his son's death (1 Samuel 2:34)

8. a baby lying in a manger (Luke 2:12)

 GET FIRED UP!

Test your knowledge with these questions about fire in the Bible.

1. What two cities were destroyed by fire coming down from heaven?

2. Why did Abraham build a fire on top of Mount Moriah?

3. What was Moses doing when God spoke to him in flames of fire coming from a bush?

4. What purpose did the pillar of fire serve as the Israelites traveled through the desert?

5. On what mountain did the Lord descend in fire?

6. Why did the Lord consume Korah and 250 of his followers with fire?

7. What had Elijah done to his offering before the fire of the Lord fell and burned it all up?

8. Who was being protected when God twice sent fire from heaven to consume a captain and his fifty men?

9. Whose servant was enabled to see the hills full of horses and chariots of fire protecting his master?

10. In the Book of Revelation, what death is the lake of fire?

GET FIRED UP!

1. Sodom and Gomorrah (Genesis 19:24)

2. He was going to sacrifice Isaac. (Genesis 22:6, 7)

3. He was tending his father-in-law's sheep. (Exodus 3:1–3)

4. It guided them. (Exodus 13:21)

5. Sinai (Exodus 19:18)

6. They rebelled against Moses, thereby treating the Lord with contempt. (Numbers 16:35)

7. He poured water all over it. (1 Kings 18:33–35)

8. Elijah (2 Kings 1:10–12)

9. Elisha's (2 Kings 6:17)

10. the second death (Revelation 21:8)

TOUCHED BY AN ANGEL

Answer these questions about Biblical figures who came into contact with angels.

1. Who had a vision of four chariots driven by angels?

2. Who did two angels rescue from the condemned city of Sodom?

3. Who did an angel send to Gaza?

4. What man did an angel take care of after he escaped the tyranny of Queen Jezebel?

5. To whom did an angel appear, bearing instructions for destroying Jericho?

6. Whose mother was visited by an angel who predicted that her son would be a Nazarite?

7. Whose donkey was frightened off the road by a vision of an angel brandishing a sword?

8. Which angel appeared to Zacharias?

9. Who was attended to by angels after he fasted in the desert?

10. Who is the only person in the Bible said to have physically wrestled with an angel?

TOUCHED BY AN ANGEL

1. Zechariah (Zechariah 6:1)

2. Lot (Genesis 19)

3. Philip (Acts 8:26)

4. Elijah (1 Kings 19)

5. Joshua (Joshua 5:13–15)

6. Samson (Jude 13:3, 4)

7. Balaam of Moab (Numbers 22:21–27)

8. Gabriel (Luke 1:19)

9. Jesus (Matthew 4:11)

10. Jacob (Genesis 32:22–32)

 MORE ON ANGELS

Identify the person associated with each of the following angel activities. (Choices: Paul, Mary, Joseph, Jesus, shepherds, Cornelius, John, Peter, George, Herod, Daniel)

1. An angel explained his vision of a ram and a goat.

2. An angel told him about the death of Herod.

3. He was strengthened by an angel during a difficult time in prayer.

4. He was instructed by an angel to send for the apostle Peter.

5. He was encouraged by an angel during a fierce storm.

6. An angel encouraged this woman's husband to marry her.

7. His plot to kill a child was foiled by an angel.

8. They heard about Jesus' birth through an angel.

9. He was freed from prison after an angel struck him on the side to awaken him.

10. An angel showed him the punishment of the great prostitute.

MORE ON ANGELS

1. Daniel (Daniel 8:16–22)

2. Joseph (Matthew 2:19, 20)

3. Jesus (Luke 22:43)

4. Cornelius (Acts 10:3)

5. Paul (Acts 27:23)

6. Mary (Matthew 1:20)

7. Herod (Matthew 2:13)

8. shepherds (Luke 2:9–14)

9. Peter (Acts 12:7)

10. John (Revelation 17:1)

KNOW THE COMPETITION

Identify the foreign gods who are described in the following statements. (Choices: Hermes, Nisroch, Artemis, Zeus, Rimmon, Mercury, Molech, the golden calf, Dagon, Asherah, Baal)

1. People erected a pole as a symbol of this female Canaanite goddess.

2. The struggle between Jehovah and this chief deity of Canaan came to a climax on Mount Carmel under Elijah.

3. Samson destroyed the temple of this Philistine god, and later the ark of God destroyed a statue of this god in its own temple.

4. Business people of Ephesus were afraid this goddess would be robbed of her divine majesty if the apostle Paul was allowed to continue his preaching.

5. The crowd in Lystra thought Barnabas was this Greek god.

6. The crowd in Lystra thought Paul was this other Greek god because he was the chief speaker.

7. Both King Ahaz and his grandson Manasseh sacrificed their children to this Ammonite god.

8. Aaron made this god on the plains of Sinai.

9. Naaman asked Elisha to forgive him for bowing down with his master to this Aramean deity.

KNOW THE COMPETITION

1. Asherah (Judges 6:25, 26)

2. Baal (1 Kings 18:16–39)

3. Dagon (Judges 16:23–30; 1 Samuel 5:1–4)

4. Artemis (Acts 19: 23–27)

5. Zeus (Acts 14:12)

6. Hermes (Acts 14:12, 13)

7. Molech (2 Kings 23:10; 2 Chronicles 28:3; 2 Chronicles 33:6)

8. the golden calf (Exodus 32)

9. Rimmon (2 Kings 5:18)

XIII

SCOUNDRELS, JAILBIRDS, AND OTHER BAD GUYS

FOOLING AROUND

Don't fool around! Fill in the blanks in these quotes about fools.

1. "The fool says in his heart that there is no _____."

2. "May my lord pay no attention to that wicked man _____. He is just like his name—his name is Fool, and folly goes with him."

3. "A fool spurns his _____ discipline."

4. "But everyone who hears these words of mine and does not put them into practice is like a foolish man who built his house on _____."

5. "Then _____ said, 'I have sinned. Come back, David my son. Because you considered my life precious today, I will not try to harm you again. Surely I have acted like a fool.'"

6. "But anyone who says, 'You fool!' will be in danger of the _____ of _____."

7. "We are fools for _____."

8. "You foolish _____! Who has bewitched you? Before your very eyes Jesus Christ was clearly portrayed as crucified."

9. "But God said to him, 'You _____! This very night your life will be demanded from you.'"

10. "Like a lame man's legs that hang limp is a _____ in the mouth of a fool."

FOOLING AROUND

1. God (Psalm 14:1)

2. Nabal (1 Samuel 25:25)

3. father's (Proverbs 15:5)

4. sand (Matthew 7:26)

5. Saul (1 Samuel 26:21)

6. fires of hell (Matthew 5:22)

7. Christ (1 Corinthians 4:10)

8. Galatian (Galatians 3:1)

9. fool (Luke 12:20) Good guess!

10. proverb (Proverbs 26:7)

WHO, ME?

Identify the Bible people who gave the following excuses (or reasons) for their actions.

1. "I told them, 'Whoever has any gold jewelry, take it off.' Then they gave me the gold, and I threw it into the fire, and out came this calf!"

2. "It is not our custom here to give the younger daughter in marriage before the older one. Finish this daughter's bridal week; then we will give you the younger one also, in return for another seven years of work."

3. "The serpent deceived me, and I ate."

4. "O Lord, I have never been eloquent, neither in the past nor since you have spoken to your servant. I am slow of speech and tongue."

5. "When I saw that the men were scattering, and that you did not come at the set time, and that the Philistines were assembling at Micmash, I thought, 'Now the Philistines will come down against me at Gilgal, and I have not sought the Lord's favor.' So I felt compelled to offer the burnt offering."

6. "But I can't flee to the mountains; this disaster will overtake me, and I'll die."

7. "Ah, Sovereign Lord, I do not know how to speak; I am only a child."

8. "Why were you searching for me? Didn't you know I had to be in my Father's house?"

WHO, ME?

1. Aaron (Exodus 32:24)

2. Laban (Genesis 29:26)

3. Eve (Genesis 3:13)

4. Moses (Exodus 4:10)

5. Saul (1 Samuel 13:11, 12)

6. Lot (Genesis 19:19)

7. Jeremiah (Jeremiah 1:6)

8. Jesus (Luke 2:49)

 LIAR, LIAR!

Can you answer these questions about Biblical liars?

1. Who told the first lie?

2. Who told his wife to lie to Pharaoh?

3. Who lied to God about laughing?

4. What did Jacob lie to his father to obtain?

5. Jacob woke up in bed with the wrong wife because he was deceived by whom?

6. Who did Potiphar's wife falsely accuse of making sport of her?

7. Who was Rahab protecting when she lied to the search party in Jericho?

8. Who lied to the Philistine Achish about the locations of his raiding expedition?

9. To trick her father, Saul, what did Michal put goats' hair on?

10. Who did Ananias and Sapphira lie to?

LIAR, LIAR!

1. Satan (Genesis 3:4)

2. Abraham (Genesis 12:13)

3. Sarah (Genesis 18:15)

4. a blessing (Genesis 27:19)

5. Laban (Genesis 29: 18–24)

6. Joseph (Genesis 39:17)

7. the spies (Joshua 2:4)

8. David (1 Samuel 27:10)

9. an idol (1 Samuel 19: 13–17)

10. the Holy Spirit (Acts 5:3)

TRUE CONFESSIONS

Can you identify the speakers of the following confessions?

1. "My ears had heard of you but now my eyes have seen you. Therefore, I despise myself and repent in dust and ashes."

2. "Father, I have sinned against heaven and against you. I am no longer worthy to be called your son."

3. "After he had counted the fighting men, he said to the Lord, 'I have sinned greatly in what I have done. Now, O Lord, I beg you, take away the guilt of your servant.'"

4. "This is what I have done: When I saw in the plunder a beautiful robe from Babylonia, two hundred shekels of silver . . . I coveted them and took them."

5. "I have sinned for I have betrayed innocent blood."

6. "I have sinned. Come back, David my son. . . . Surely I have acted like a fool and have erred greatly."

7. "Oh, what a great sin these people have committed! They have made themselves gods of gold."

8. "I have sinned against the Lord your God and against you. Now forgive my sin once more and pray to the Lord your God to take this deadly plague away from me."

9. "Let us lie down in our shame, and let our disgrace cover us. We have sinned against the Lord our God."

10. "She (Tamar) is more righteous than I, since I wouldn't give her to my son Shelah."

TRUE CONFESSIONS

1. Job (Job 42:5, 6)

2. the prodigal son (Luke 15:21)

3. David (2 Samuel 24:10)

4. Achan (Joshua 7:20, 21)

5. Judas (Matthew 27:4)

6. Saul (1 Samuel 26:21)

7. Moses (Exodus 32:31)

8. Pharaoh (Exodus 10:16, 17)

9. Jeremiah (Jeremiah 3:25)

10. Judah (Genesis 38:26)

MURDER AND MAYHEM

On the left is a list of killers, and on the right, their unfortunate victims. Can you match the slayer and slain?

1. ___ Ehud   a. an Egyptian

2. ___ Moses   b. Abel

3. ___ Joab   c. Goliath

4. ___ David   d. the entire army of Pharaoh

5. ___ Recab and Baanah   e. Abner

6. ___ Simeon and Levi   f. Hamor and Shechem

7. ___ Cain   g. a thousand men

8. ___ Samson   h. Ish-Bosheth

9. ___ Abishai   i. three hundred soldiers

10. ___ Red Sea   j. King Eglon of Moab

MURDER AND MAYHEM

1. j. King Eglon of Moab (Judges 3:21)

2. a. an Egyptian (Exodus 2:12)

3. e. Abner (2 Samuel 3:27)

4. c. Goliath (1 Samuel 17:51)

5. h. Ish-Bosheth (2 Samuel 4:6)

6. f. Hamor and Shechem (Genesis 34:26)

7. b. Abel (Genesis 4:8)

8. g. a thousand men (Judges 15:15)

9. i. three hundred soldiers (2 Samuel 23:18)

10. d. the entire army of Pharaoh (Exodus 14:28)

JUST DESERTS

On the left is a list of Bible characters, and on the right, the punishments they received. Can you match the person with his punishment?

1. ___ Paul   a. thrown into the fire

2. ___ Zechariah   b. death by the sword

3. ___ Haman   c. stoned to death

4. ___ Samson   d. forty lashes, minus one

5. ___ Shadrach   e. put in the stocks

6. ___ Satan   f. exiled

7. ___ John   g. hanged

8. ___ Daniel   h. blinded

9. ___ Agag   i. thrown into a lake of fire

10. ___ Jeremiah   j. thrown to the lions

JUST DESERTS

1. d. forty lashes, minus one (2 Corinthians 11:24)

2. c. stoned to death (2 Chronicles 24:21)

3. g. hanged (Esther 7:10)

4. h. blinded (Judges 16:21)

5. a. thrown into the fire (Daniel 3:1)

6. i. thrown into a lake of fire (Revelation 20:10)

7. f. exiled (Revelation 1:9)

8. j. thrown to the lions (Daniel 6:16)

9. b. death by the sword (1 Samuel 15:33)

10. e. put in the stocks (Jeremiah 20:2)

 IN THE SLAMMER

Identify the person described in each of the following prison situations.
(Choices: Jesus, Silas, Samson, Jeremiah, Peter, John the Baptist,
Simeon, Zedekiah, Hercules, Satan, Joseph)

1. The lies of Potiphar's wife landed this man in prison.

2. Herod seized this man and threw him into prison in order to please the Jews.

3. This man said that when people visited the least of his brothers in prison they visited him.

4. Paul and this man prayed and sang hymns together in prison.

5. This poor guy had his eyes gouged out, his legs bound with bronze shackles, and was set to grinding in prison.

6. This man's prison was a cistern.

7. This man was imprisoned because Herod disliked his advice on marriage.

8. He was imprisoned in order to make sure his brothers would return.

9. This man's eyes were put out; he was bound with bronze shackles, and sent off to prison in Babylon.

10. His prison sentence will last one thousand years.

IN THE SLAMMER

1. Joseph (Genesis 39:20–23)

2. Peter (Acts 12:4)

3. Jesus (Matthew 27:40)

4. Silas (Acts 16:23)

5. Samson (Judges 16:21, 22)

6. Jeremiah (Jeremiah 38)

7. John the Baptist (Matthew 14:3–12)

8. Simeon (Genesis 42:24)

9. Zedekiah (Jeremiah 39:7)

10. Satan (Revelation 20:3)

 GREAT ESCAPES

Can you answer these questions about Biblical escapes?

1. Who left Gath and escaped to the cave of Adullam?

2. Who escaped from Sodom and Gomorrah before God destroyed them with burning sulfur from heaven?

3. What was David doing when he escaped Saul's attempt to pin him to the wall with a spear?

4. Who or what helped Peter escape from a Roman prison?

5. What happened to the man who escaped from battle in order to report to David the death of Saul?

6. Who heard this report: "The fire of God fell from the sky and burned up the sheep and the servants, and I am the only one who has escaped to tell you!"?

7. Before his escape, what were the furious people in Nazareth going to do with Jesus?

8. When the jailer realized that Paul and Silas might have escaped, what did he do?

9. Paul said that because God is faithful, he will always provide people a way to escape what?

10. Paul hoped that those who opposed Timothy would come to their senses and escape the trap of what?

GREAT ESCAPES

1. David (I Samuel 22:1)

2. Lot (Genesis 19:23, 24)

3. He was playing his harp. (1 Samuel 18:9–11)

4. an angel (Acts 12:7)

5. David had him killed. (2 Samuel 1:15)

6. Job (Job 1:16)

7. throw him over the cliff (Luke 4:29, 30)

8. He was about to kill himself. (Acts 16:27)

9. temptation (1 Corinthians 10:13)

10. the devil (2 Timothy 2:26)

DEMONS, DEVILS, AND WITCHES

Answer these questions about various bad guys in the Bible.

1. What happened to the demons Jesus cast out of the two men in the region of the Gadarenes?

2. What was the demon-possessed man able to do after Jesus cast his demon out?

3. How many demons did Jesus drive out of Mary Magdalene?

4. What was the penalty in Israel for consulting mediums and spiritists?

5. What happened when King Saul asked the witch of Endor to bring up Samuel from the dead?

6. What did Paul tell the people of Ephesus to wear in order to withstand the devil's schemes?

7. To whom did Jesus say, "Get behind me, Satan! You are a stumbling block to me"?

8. Before Paul healed her, how did the demon-possessed slave girl in Philippi make money for her owners?

DEMONS, DEVILS, AND WITCHES

1. They went into a herd of pigs. (Matthew 8:28–34)

2. He could speak. (Matthew 9:32, 33)

3. seven (Luke 8:2)

4. to be cut off from the people (Leviticus 20:6)

5. Samuel came up. (1 Samuel 28:12–19)

6. the armor of God (Ephesians 6:11)

7. Peter (Matthew 16:23)

8. by telling fortunes (Acts 16:16)

THE ULTIMATE SCOUNDREL

In the following quotes, fill in the blanks to complete the names and titles for the Devil. (The first letter of each missing word has been provided for you.)

1. "Then S_____ entered Judas Iscariot, one of the twelve."

2. "You followed the ways of this world and of the r_____ of the kingdom of the air."

3. "The g_____ of this a_____ has blinded the minds of unbelievers."

4. "Now the p_____ of this w_____ will be driven out."

5. "The great d_____ was hurled down—that ancient serpent called the devil."

6. "They had as king over them the a_____ of the A_____, whose name in Hebrew is Abaddon, and in Greek, Apollyon."

7. "They said, 'It is only by B_____, the prince of demons, that this fellow drives out demons.'"

8. "What harmony is there between Christ and B_____?"

9. "He was a m_____ from the beginning, not holding to the truth, for there is no truth in him."

10. "Satan himself masquerades as an a_____ of l_____."

THE ULTIMATE SCOUNDREL

1. Satan (Luke 22:3)

2. ruler (Ephesians 2:2)

3. god of this age (2 Corinthians 4:4)

4. prince of this world (John 12:31)

5. dragon (Revelation 12:9)

6. angel of the Abyss (Revelation 9:11)

7. Beelzebub (Matthew 12:24)

8. Belial (2 Corinthians 6:15)

9. murderer (John 8:44)

10. angel of light (2 Corinthians 11:14, 15)

XIV

FAMOUS
FINISHES

 FAMOUS LAST WORDS

Before they died, who spoke these famous last words?

1. "Let me die with the Philistines!"

2. "God will surely come to your aid, and then you must carry my bones up from this place."

3. "Draw your sword and run me through, or these uncircumcised fellows will come and run me through and abuse me."

4. "Lord, do not hold this sin against them."

5. "You should have struck the ground five or six times; then you would have defeated Aram and completely destroyed it. But now you will defeat it only three times."

6. "See! This stone . . . will be a witness against you if you are untrue to your God."

7. "There I buried Leah. The field and the cave in it were bought from the Hittites."

8. "You are a man of wisdom; you will know what to do to him. Bring his gray head down to the grave in blood."

9. "Blessed are you, O Israel! Who is like you, a people saved by the Lord? He is your shield and helper and your glorious sword. Your enemies will cower before you, and you will trample down their high places."

10. "It is finished."

FAMOUS LAST WORDS

1. Samson (Judges 16:30)

2. Joseph (Genesis 50:25)

3. Saul (1 Samuel 31:4)

4. Stephen (Acts 7:60)

5. Elisha (2 Kings 13:19)

6. Joshua (Joshua 24:27)

7. Jacob (Genesis 49:31, 32)

8. David (1 Kings 2:9)

9. Moses (Deuteronomy 33:29)

10. Jesus (John 19:30)

 DON'T MESS WITH GOD

Identify these people and places that got on God's bad side, and so met their bitter end.

1.   This city was destroyed because of its gross immorality.

2.   This man, Judah's firstborn and husband to Tamar, was put to death because he was so wicked.

3.   The brother of Er refused to produce offspring with Tamar, so God put him to death.

4.   Fire came out from the presence of the Lord and consumed these two sons of Aaron.

5.   Doing this activity on the Sabbath day resulted in a man being stoned to death.

6.   This is how Korah, Dathan, and Abiram were punished for rebelling against the authority of Moses.

7.   The Lord sent these among the Israelites to kill them because they had spoken against God.

8.   Uzzah was struck down because he touched something when the oxen stumbled.

9.   The prophet Hananiah died for this reason.

10. This king had James executed, and was himself struck down for not giving praise to God.

DON'T MESS WITH GOD

1. Sodom (Genesis 19:27–29)

2. Er (Genesis 38:7)

3. Onan (Genesis 38:10)

4. Nadab and Abihu (Leviticus 10:2)

5. gathering wood (Numbers 15:32–36)

6. The earth opened up and swallowed them. (Numbers 16:31, 32)

7. venomous snakes (Numbers 21:6)

8. the ark of God (2 Samuel 6:7)

9. He was a false prophet. (Jeremiah 28:15–17)

10. Herod (Acts 12:23)

STRANGE WAYS TO DIE

On the left is a list of Bible people, and on the right, the way they died. Can you match each person with his unfortunate end?

1. ___ Herod

2. ___ John the Baptist

3. ___ Saul

4. ___ Absalom

5. ___ Sisera

6. ___ Judas

7. ___ Abimelech

8. ___ Jesus

9. ___ Eli

10. ___ Haman

a. was crucified

b. fell backward off his chair and broke his neck

c. was beheaded

d. was eaten by worms

e. was hung on the gallows he had prepared for someone else

f. had three javelins plunged into his heart

g. had a tent peg driven through his temple

h. fell on his sword

i. hung himself, body burst open, intestines spilled out

j. a millstone dropped on his head

STRANGE WAYS TO DIE

1. d. was eaten by worms (Acts 12:23)

2. c. was beheaded (Matthew 14:10)

3. h. fell on his sword (1 Samuel 31:4)

4. f. had three javelins plunged into his heart (2 Samuel 18:14)

5. g. had a tent peg driven into his temple (Judges 4:21)

6. i. hung himself, body burst open, intestines spilled out (Matthew 27:5; Acts 1:18)

7. j. a millstone dropped on his head (Judges 9:53)

8. a. was crucified (Matthew 27:35)

9. b. fell backward off his chair and broke his neck (1 Samuel 4:18)

10. e. was hung on the gallows he had prepared for someone else (Esther 7:10)

THAT'S DISGUSTING!

True or false? Did these disgusting things really happen in the Bible?

1. A man cut up the body of his concubine limb by limb into twelve parts, and sent them into all the areas of Israel.

2. A woman was thrown from a window, and her blood spattered a wall and the horses as they trampled her underfoot.

3. On his way to his wedding, a man stopped by the side of the road to eat honey from the carcass of a dead lion.

4. A group of Philistines ate a meal using as bowls the heads of twelve camels.

5. An Israelite plunged his sword into a Moabite so hard that the blade came out his back, and his fat closed over the handle.

6. A rebellious Israelite was decapitated by the branch of an oak tree as he fled in his chariot from his pursuers.

7. A man was chewed into small pieces by a great fish and then spit out on the beach of Nineveh.

8. Joab plunged his dagger into Amasa's belly, and his intestines spilled out on the ground.

9. The prophets of Baal cut off their fingers and toes, hoping to induce their god to ignite the wood of their sacrifice on Mount Carmel.

10. During a birthday party, a woman was presented with the head of her enemy on a platter.

THAT'S DISGUSTING!

1. True (Judges 19:29)

2. True (2 Kings 9:33)

3. True (Judges 14:8)

4. False

5. True (Judges 3: 21, 22)

6. False

7. False

8. True (2 Samuel 20:10)

9. False

10. True (Matthew 14:6–11)

DEAD OR ALIVE?

Fill in the blanks to complete the following statement about people who died, almost died, died and came back, or didn't die at all.

1. When Jesus called _____ out from the grave, he emerged still wrapped in grave clothes.

2. _____ brought back to life the dead son of a Shunammite woman by lying upon the boy.

3. Jesus brought back to life the daughter of _____.

4. It was said of _____, "He walked with God; then he was no more, because God took him away."

5. Peter raised back to life a woman named _____, who was known for doing good works and helping the poor.

6. _____ was in a tomb for three days before God raised him.

7. _____ cried out to the Lord, and the son of the woman of Zarephath was brought back to life.

8. Jesus visited the town of _____ and there raised to life the dead son of a widow.

9. The body of a dead man was thrown into the tomb of _____, and when the body touched the bones, the man came back to life.

10. _____ never died; he was taken up to heaven in a whirlwind.

DEAD OR ALIVE?

1. Lazarus (John 11:43, 44)

2. Elisha (2 Kings 4:33–35)

3. Jairus (Mark 5:22–43)

4. Enoch (Genesis 5:24)

5. Dorcas (Acts 9:36–42)

6. Jesus (John 20)

7. Elijah (1 Kings 17:22)

8. Nain (Luke 7:11–15)

9. Elisha (2 Kings 13:20, 21)

10. Elijah (2 Kings 2:11)

GOOD HEAVENLY DAYS!

Answer these questions about the place where everyone wants to end up—heaven!

1. According to Jesus in the Beatitudes, who is blessed "for theirs is the kingdom of heaven"?

2. Who is preparing a place in heaven for the disciples?

3. To whom did Jesus say, "Today, you will be with me in paradise"?

4. Jesus tells Nicodemus that something must be true of anyone who wants to see the kingdom of God. What is it?

5. Who said: "Look, I see heaven open and the Son of Man standing at the right hand of God"?

6. Whose voice will accompany Jesus' descent from heaven in the last days?

7. Paul writes to the Corinthians about a man who was caught up to which heaven?

8. What does Paul tell the Philippians that they have in heaven?

9. The two angels told the disciples that Jesus would return in what manner?

GOOD HEAVENLY DAYS!

1. the poor in spirit (Matthew 5:3)

2. Jesus (John 14:2)

3. the thief on the cross (Luke 23:43)

4. They must be born again. (John 3:3)

5. Stephen (Acts 7:56)

6. the archangel's (1 Thessalonians 4:16)

7. the third (2 Corinthians 12:2)

8. their citizenship (Philippians 3:20)

9. the same way he left (Acts 1:11)

THE HOT SPOT

In these Biblical quotes, fill in the blanks with words or phrases used to describe the place where no one wants to end up—hell. (The first letter of each missing word has been provided.)

1. "They will be thrown into the f_____ f_____."

2. "On this rock I will build my church, and the gates of H_____ will not overcome it."

3. "If anyone's name was not found written in the book of life, he was thrown into the l_____ of f_____."

4. "For if you remain silent, I will be like those who have gone down to the p_____."

5. "And they begged him repeatedly not to order them to go into the A_____."

6. "Throw that worthless servant outside, into the darkness, where there will be w_____ and g_____ of teeth."

7. "It is better for you to enter the kingdom of God with one eye than to have two eyes and be thrown into hell, where 'their w_____ does not die, and the f_____ is not quenched.'"

8. "They who seek my life will be destroyed; they will go down to the d_____ of the e_____."

285

THE HOT SPOT

1. fiery furnace (Matthew 13:42)

2. Hades (Matthew 16:18)

3. lake of fire (Revelation 20:15)

4. pit (Psalm 28:1)

5. Abyss (Luke 8:31)

6. weeping and gnashing (Matthew 25:30)

7. worm does not die, and the fire is not quenched (Mark 9:48)

8. depths of the earth (Psalm 63:9)

 IT IS FINISHED

Can you name the books of the Bible that end with the following lines?

1. "Give her the reward she has earned, and let her works bring her praise at the city gate."

2. "Jesus did many other things as well."

3. "And the name of the city from that time on will be: 'The Lord is there.'"

4. "So Joseph died at the age of a hundred and ten."

5. "Amen. Come, Lord Jesus. The grace of the Lord Jesus be with God's people. Amen."

6. "These are the commands and regulations the Lord gave through Moses to the Israelites on the plains of Moab by the Jordan across from Jericho."

7. "My love to all of you in Christ Jesus. Amen."

8. "Day by day the king of Babylon gave Jehoiachin a regular allowance as long as he lived, till the day of his death."

9. "Then they worshiped him and returned to Jerusalem with great joy. And they stayed continually at the temple, praising God."

10. "Dear children, keep yourselves from idols."

IT IS FINISHED

1. Proverbs

2. John

3. Ezekiel

4. Genesis

5. Revelation

6. Numbers

7. 1 Corinthians

8. Jeremiah

9. Luke

10. 1 John

XV

THE
BIBLE
TODAY

STRAIGHT TO THE SOURCE:
Old Testament

The following statements describe frequently used words and phrases that originated in the Old Testament. Can you name the words and phrases?s

1. This is something that ruins a situation that is otherwise perfect.

2. A noisy confusion of many voices, sounds, or languages is sometimes labeled with this word.

3. This phrase is used to describe a situation in which there are signs warning of imminent danger, failure, or collapse.

4. People use this phrase to refer to someone they cherish.

5. This phrase is used to describe something that is unimportant when compared with other concerns.

6. Equality between the crime and the punishment is referred to with this phrase.

7. A person who tries to comfort another but actually makes them feel worse is called by this phrase.

8. This word is used to describe a special anniversary; for example, a fiftieth anniversary.

9. A person who takes the blame for the wrongdoing of others is called this.

10. If a person escapes some danger by the narrowest of margins, their escape is described with this phrase.

STRAIGHT TO THE SOURCE:
Old Testament

Citations were taken from the King James version of the Bible.

1. a fly in the ointment (Ecclesiastes 10:1)

2. Babel (Genesis 11:1–9)

3. the writing is on the wall (Daniel 5)

4. the apple of one's eye (Deuteronomy 32:10)

5. a drop in the bucket (Isaiah 40:15)

6. an eye for an eye (Exodus 21:22–24)

7. Job's comforter (Job 16:2)

8. jubilee (Leviticus 25:8–17)

9. a scapegoat (Leviticus 16:8)

10. by the skin of their teeth (Job 19:20)

STRAIGHT TO THE SOURCE:
New Testament

The following statements describe frequently used words and phrases that originated in the New Testament. Can you name the words and phrases?

1. To do this is to ignore or not retaliate for an insult or injury.

2. This phrase is used to describe a situation in which an ignorant or inexperienced person is directing someone who is equally ignorant or inexperienced.

3. To do this is to give something valuable to someone who is unable or unwilling to show appreciation.

4. A skeptic is often referred to with this phrase.

5. This phrase refers to a person who helps people in need.

6. Someone who conceals their good deeds, character, or talents from others is said to do this.

7. This phrase is used to describe a person's decision that they will have nothing more to do with a situation.

8. People with wholesome character and solid values are sometimes described with this phrase.

9. People who follow a literal and strict interpretation of rules are said to follow this.

10. If a cruel and dangerous person is pretending to be good and harmless, they can be described with this phrase.

STRAIGHT TO THE SOURCE:
New Testament

Citations were taken from the King James version of the Bible.

1. turn the other cheek (Matthew 5:39)

2. the blind leading the blind (Matthew 15:14)

3. cast pearls before swine (Matthew 7:6)

4. doubting Thomas (John 20:24–29)

5. good Samaritan (Luke 10:30–37)

6. hide one's light under a bushel (Matthew 5:15)

7. wash one's hands of something (Matthew 27:24)

8. salt of the earth (Matthew 5:13, 14)

9. the letter of the law (2 Corinthians 3:5, 6)

10. a wolf in sheep's clothing (Matthew 7:15)

PROBLEM PROVERBS

True or false? Decide which of the following popular adages actually came from the Bible.

1. "Do not add insult to injury."

2. "The fear of the Lord is the beginning of knowledge."

3. "Discretion is the better part of valor."

4. "Beware of Greeks bearing gifts."

5. "Leave no stone unturned."

6. "Do unto others as you would have them do unto you."

7. "Where your treasure is, there your heart will be also."

8. "Do not look a gift horse in the mouth."

9. "Pride goes before a fall."

10. "A little learning is a dangerous thing."

PROBLEM PROVERBS

1. False

2. True (Proverbs 1:7)

3. False

4. False

5. False

6. True (Matthew 7:12)

7. True (Matthew 6:21)

8. False

9. True (Proverbs 16:18)

10. False

MORE PROBLEM PROVERBS

True or false? Decide which of the following adages actually came from the Bible and which did not.

1. "Let your 'Yes' be 'Yes' and your 'No,' 'No.'"

2. "God helps those who help themselves."

3. "Do not judge, or you too will be judged."

4. "Do as you would be done by."

5. "There but for the grace of God go I."

6. "A bird in the hand is worth two in the bush."

7. "He who spares the rod hates his son."

8. "The love of money is a root of all kinds of evil."

9. "Cleanliness is next to godliness."

10. "There is a time for everything, and a season for every activity under heaven."

MORE PROBLEM PROVERBS

1.   True (Matthew 5:37)

2.   False

3.   True (Matthew 7:1)

4.   False

5.   False

6.   False

7.   True (Proverbs 13:24)

8.   True (1 Timothy 6:10)

9.   False

10.   True (Ecclesiastes 3:1)

SPORTS TRIVIA IN THE BIBLE

Identify these famous sports figures using the hints from the Bible.

1. He holds the major league career record of 755 home runs, and he shares his last name with Moses' brother.

2. He holds the record for most points scored in an NBA playoff game (63), and his first name is the name of an angel and his last of a river in the Bible.

3. He holds the NBA career record for assists, and he shares his first name with a disciple who wrote a Gospel.

4. This swimmer won seven gold medals in 1972 in Munich, and he also shares his first name with the writer of one of the Gospels.

5. This track star set six world records in 45 minutes on May 25, 1935, and he shares his first name with King David's father.

6. He holds the major league record for most runs scored in a season, and he shares his last name with King David's great-grandmother.

7. This baseball player holds the major league record for career base hits, and his last name is the same as the famous flower of Sharon.

8. She has won more tennis titles than any other woman, and she shares her last name with two books of the Bible.

9. He was the NBA's Most Valuable Player for the 1995 season, and he shares his first name with one of Israel's kings.

SPORTS TRIVIA IN THE BIBLE

1.   Hank *Aaron* (Exodus 4:14)

2.   *Michael Jordan* (Daniel 10:13; Genesis 13:10)

3.   *John* Stockton (the Gospel of John)

4.   *Mark* Spitz (the Gospel of Mark)

5.   *Jesse* Owens (1 Samuel 16)

6.   Babe *Ruth* (Ruth 4:18–22)

7.   Pete *Rose* (Song of Songs 2:1)

8.   Billie Jean *King* (1 and 2 Kings)

9.   *David* Robinson (1 Samuel 16)

 GO, TEAM, GO!

Identify these professional sports teams by using hints from the Bible.

1. The creature for which this team is named was presented at the entrance of the Tent of Meeting as a sin offering.

2. This team is named after "ministering spirits sent to serve those who will inherit salvation."

3. This team is named after the sons of Rebekah.

4. This football team is named after the birds that fed Elijah while he hid in the Kerith Ravine.

5. The descendants of a Philistine named Rapha were described like this; so are a West Coast baseball team and an East Coast football team.

6. This hockey team is named after the ultimate bad boy.

7. This football team would like to soar on wings like a particular bird—"they will run and not grow weary."

8. This football team uses the name that the apostle Paul used to describe the believers in Rome and other cities.

9. This southern basketball team shares its name with the annoying critters that God sent ahead of Joshua's army to drive out the inhabitants of the land.

10. Solomon lined the steps leading to his throne with statues of these creatures, whose name is shared by a football team.

GO, TEAM, GO!

1. Chicago *Bulls* (Leviticus 4:1–4)

2. Anaheim *Angels* (Hebrews 1:14)

3. Minnesota *Twins* (Genesis 25:24)

4. Baltimore *Ravens* (1 Kings 17:5, 6)

5. San Francisco and New York *Giants* (2 Samuel 21:15–22)

6. New Jersey *Devils* (1 Peter 5:8)

7. Philadelphia *Eagles* (Isaiah 40:31)

8. New Orleans *Saints* (Romans 1:7)

9. Charlotte *Hornets* (Joshua 24:12)

10. Detroit *Lions* (1 Kings 10:20)

GOING TO THE MOVIES

Can you identify these movies by using hints from the Bible?

1. This film won Best Picture in 1981, and its title comes from a phrase in a Bible story about Elisha.

2. Satan is called the angel of this place, which is also the title of a 1989 movie starring Ed Harris.

3. He was one of King Solomon's district governors, and his name was the title of this 1959 Academy Award winner.

4. The central object of this 1981 film starring Harrison Ford was the chest containing the Ten Commandments.

5. Could the title of this 1954 musical have been taken from Jesus' conversation with the Sadducees about a woman who died after being married many times?

6. This classic starring Bette Davis won several Academy Awards, and its title includes the name of Seth's mother.

7. This 1949 comedy starring Spencer Tracy and Katharine Hepburn is named for the source from which God made Eve.

8. This 1924 silent film was named after a vice that the apostle Paul says is the same as idolatry.

9. Robert Redford starred in this 1972 film, whose title includes the name of an Old Testament prophet.

10. This film got James Dean started, and its title is a phrase in the Bible about the place where history got started.

GOING TO THE MOVIES

1. *Chariots of Fire* (2 Kings 6:17)

2. *The Abyss* (Revelation 9:11)

3. *Ben-Hur* (1 Kings 4:8)

4. *Raiders of the Lost Ark* (Exodus 25)

5. *Seven Brides for Seven Brothers* (Matthew 22:23–32)

6. *All About Eve* (Genesis 5:3)

7. *Adam's Rib* (Genesis 2:22)

8. *Greed* (Colossians 3:5)

9. *Jeremiah Johnson* (Jeremiah)

10. *East of Eden* (Genesis 4:24)

STAR-STRUCK

Can you identify these movie stars by using hints from the Bible?

1. This movie star won Best Actor for his part in *Yankee Doodle Dandy*, and he shares his first name with the writer of a New Testament letter.

2. *Lawrence of Arabia* was this actor's first major film role, and he shares his first name with the apostle Andrew's brother.

3. He starred in *Butch Cassidy and the Sundance Kid* and shares his first name with the greatest evangelist in the New Testament.

4. He finally won an Oscar for *True Grit*, and he shares his first name with one of the Gospel writers.

5. This actress's first name is found in the salutations of many of Paul's letters—a word that means "a virtue coming from God."

6. This star of the 1989 movie *My Left Foot* has the same first name as the man who refused to eat the royal food and wine served in Nebuchadnezzar's court.

7. He starred in *The Guns of Navarone*, and he shares his first name with a famous king of Israel.

8. This famous star of *National Velvet* shares her first name with John the Baptist's mother.

9. One of the Gospel writers has the same first name as this star of the 1988 comedy *Biloxi Blues*.

10. This actor/comedian often starred with Bing Crosby, and his last name is one of the apostle Paul's three cardinal virtues.

STAR-STRUCK

1. *James* Cagney (James)

2. *Peter* O'Toole (Matthew 4:18)

3. *Paul* Newman (Acts 13:9)

4. *John* Wayne (John)

5. *Grace* Kelly (Ephesians 1:2)

6. *Daniel* Day-Lewis (Daniel 1:8)

7. *David* Niven (1 Samuel 16)

8. *Elizabeth* Taylor (Luke 1:57)

9. *Matthew* Broderick (Matthew)

10. Bob *Hope* (1 Corinthians 13:13)